A Force Unfamiliar to Me

A Cautionary Tale

A Force Unfamiliar to Me

A Cautionary Tale

Jane B. Butler

with
Selections from the Journals
of
Peter Brooks Butler

Acknowledgements

Although Peter's words were always my inspiration, I could not have written this memoir without the friends, relations, and professionals who were my audience and critiquers through the many drafts of my manuscript. In order of their appearance in the process I owe many thanks to my cousin Bonner Elwell, the author Ann Arensberg, typist Karen Miller, literary agent Lane Zachary, and writing instructor Peter Davies. I would also like to thank Vivian Mason of Studley Press for her care and interest in preparing my manuscript for publication.

Finally a tribute I wish she could have read to my friend, Toni Handy, who died unexpectedly last summer, for the spur of her detailed, incisive comments on each of the chapters and even pieces of chapters that I handed her over the years.

Cover design by Susan Hendrix and Studley Press
Cover photo by Carolyn B. Butler

Published by Hamlet Books, P.O. Box 667, Lenox, MA 01240
Printed by The Studley Press, Inc., Dalton, MA 01226

Dedication

For Brooks, Carolyn and Tom
And with thanks to the friends who had
the imagination and the patience to listen.

1

WHEN I CAME IN FROM THE DENTIST AND SHOPPING, THE PHONE was ringing. Peter was calling from a noisy place, the student union at Boston University, I imagined.

"What day is Dad coming to Boston?"

"Tomorrow, Wednesday."

"I think I can have dinner with him. Tell him to call me when he gets here."

I was about to call Brooks to the phone when Peter said quickly, "I gotta go now, Mom."

A few hours later, I could hear Brooks on the phone in the room above the living room. I knew it was Tom, our younger son, calling from boarding school so I started up the stairs to remind Brooks to ask him about a charge on one of the Christmas bills. As I reached the balcony, Brooks called out, "Tom says Peter sounded very bad last night."

"What time did he talk to him?"

"Eight o'clock."

As I reached the doorway I said,"You talked to him two hours later and he sounded fine. He was going up and down. That frightens me." I wasn't sure Brooks heard me as he was still talking to Tom.

When Peter had called the night before, Brooks, who

was lying on his bed, had rolled onto mine and picked up the phone. I had listened from the other side of the room. Peter was entertaining his father with details about a party he had been to on the weekend, saying something about a computer program in his journalism class and finally asking about our cat and dog. As he hung up Brooks had said, "I haven't heard Peter's voice so up in quite a while."

Now he was saying, "Tom called Carolyn and asked her to check on Peter."

I went to the kitchen phone to call Peter, then decided to see what his sister had heard from him. I reached Carolyn who said Peter had sounded okay at about eleven-thirty. But they hadn't talked long because he was tired and when she suggested a movie the next night, he said he had to study. They agreed to go together to see my parents on the weekend. It all sounded normal and I did not call Peter.

I still see myself reaching out for the green receiver on the wall, starting to dial Peter's number, dialing Carolyn's.

He did not get to the hotel that night until after eight. I could have reached him. He must have gone home to pack the soft bag that he took with him.

The next time I held that phone it was a few minutes after nine the next morning, Wednesday morning.

Two policemen, stood in my living room right where the Christmas tree had been.

One of them said, "Your son passed away in the night."

"It's Peter." Brooks' voice cut across the policeman's. He had known for seconds longer. He had been standing on the back step and had seen the police car turn in. We held onto each other for just a moment. I must have asked a question the policeman couldn't or didn't want to answer because he gave me a torn piece of paper with a number for the Boston police on it and I took it to the kitchen phone.

Someone at the Metropolitan police answered. With no delay, I was switched to someone else who told me very quickly that a Peter Butler had jumped from the Park Plaza

Hotel at 6:15 that morning. We had often stayed at the Park Plaza. Sometimes Peter was with us. Sometimes he met us there. I had sat on one of the seats which surrounded a column in the center of the large lobby and watched for him to come swinging through the revolving door.

I knew but I reached anyway for one last possibility.

"How old was he?"

The man's voice said, "Twenty-one."

Softly, almost to myself, I said, "Twenty-two." And hung up.

2

As I replaced the kitchen receiver I wanted to reverse my short journey back through the hall to the bedroom. I had been standing by the bed folding sheets when I heard the commotion in the living room. But a wall was already there and in that instant I knew sharply that I would never be on the other side of it again, that I was cut off from all retreats, from all familiar places in my mind.

I had at times in predawn waking moments wondered how I might behave if word should ever come to me of the death of one of my children and I had gone so far as to picture myself retreating to a dark room, curling up, holding the knowledge in. But in the evanescent sadness of such imaginings, there had been no wall.

I reached for the phone again, I had to tell the news of Peter's death to someone, someone who would understand but not be directly in the path of its destruction. I called Susan. She and I had had tea in town the afternoon before and talked of her son, who had died of heart disease when he was twenty-four. And she had known Peter.

The four of us, Susan and her husband, Gene, Brooks and I stood in the gray light of the kitchen for a while. I don't remember what we said, except that Susan tried to calm me, to persuade me that I did not have to call everyone immediately. Then as they left to make some local calls for us, Susan gently pointed out that my hair was still in clips. I had washed it before breakfast back on the other side of the wall. As I went down the hall, I slipped the clips out of my hair and combed it out unseeing, before I sat down on my bed and picked up the phone.

I called Carolyn's apartment and got her roommate, Liz. Cutting through her gasp I told her she would have to find her way to the Day Care center where Carolyn was working. I called my youngest sister, Isabella, who lived next door to my parents and not far from Carolyn. I knew she would have to take on the burden of telling our parents and starting the news around the family. But her line was busy. I tried several times then called the Recording for the Blind studio where I was scheduled to read. It was as though I had learned phrases in a foreign tongue, "My son committed suicide last night," or "Peter died last night; he killed himself; he jumped from the Park Plaza."

I kept dialing Isabella's number. Finally an operator responded to my insistent tone by giving me the listings for a neighboring house, but I didn't recognize any of the names as that of a friend Isabella had mentioned. I tried her number again. The line was still busy.

Peter had been dead for hours and so many people who had to know thought he was still alive. I didn't call my mother's house because I wanted someone to be with her when she was told. In spite of her age, partial blindness and arthritis, I knew she would be the first to answer the phone. My father might be out,but even when he was home he waited for my mother to answer.

At about noon Isabella finally answered. "I've been trying to reach you," I started and cutting off her explanations of who she had been talking to, I said, "Peter killed himself this morning."

I could hear her catch her breath in a long fading, "Oh."

And then the words, "It's always the sweet ones."

I told her Liz was getting Carolyn and but that our mother didn't know yet that I hadn't wanted to call her. Isabella said she would go right over to the other house.

"I feel like tearing myself in little pieces and throwing myself away." My mother's words sounded right to me. Carolyn, who was already with her came on the phone. I don't remember what we said except that Liz would drive her home to Lenox. Later, she told me that she had been in the schoolyard surrounded by children when she saw Liz coming towards her. "I knew it was something terrible, and when she told me, I started to laugh. A crazy laugh, Mom. I couldn't stop."

I can't picture where Brooks was most of that morning but at some point between my calls to Isabella, we agreed that he should call Tom's school, Westminster. He talked to someone he knew in the administration who said that one of us must tell Tom about his brother. So it was agreed that Tom be told only that he should call home because his father was driving to Hartford and would stop to take him out for lunch.

Some crazy instinct to protect Tom must have made us say that. He was given the message as he left his last class of the morning and happily watched his friends go off to lunch as he headed for the phone and the prospects of a better meal.

Ann, a friend who had come over on hearing the news from Susan, was alone in the kitchen and picked up the phone. Tom knew her voice and asked why she was there. She called out to us almost in panic. Brooks answered upstairs in the TV room just before I got to the bedroom phone. I heard him say, "Peter killed himself last night." Tom screamed. And then Brooks and I could hear each other calling his name until we realized he was no longer there.

Brooks must have come down to our bedroom because we decided to call the school infirmary. He had the number in a little address book on his bureau. We had used that number so often over the last eight years, especially when Peter was at the school and had suffered many recalcitrant infections. Mrs. Schmitz, the head nurse, had told us how much she admired him for complaining so little.

Brooks reached Mrs. Schmitz right away and Tom was with her. He had dropped the phone and run down a staircase and along a narrow hall. As he burst through the infirmary door, Mrs. Schmitz and another nurse literally caught his thin frame between them. They already knew.

"We're coming right down to get you," I told him.

"Be careful, you guys, be careful," he said.

There was no color in the sky that day and none on the campus. We drove behind the main building near the stairway to Tom's room. He appeared in the long, dark, dress coat my mother had given him for Christmas. Already there was a guarded look in his eyes. "Where did he do it?" he asked.

If Peter had been our only child, we would probably have gone to Boston, to the hotel and to the hospital. But as it was, his body, identified by dental records, was released to someone from a funeral home we had contacted in Lenox and returned sometime later that day over some of the same route we had taken with Tom.

When we got home, Ann was still there, Susan had returned and Carolyn had arrived with Liz. There were calls all evening and more people came as it got dark. Food had been brought in and, at more or less our usual hour, five of us (Liz would stay a few days) sat down to eat, leaving empty Peter's place beside his father.

We all went to bed around eleven. Just as I was pulling up the covers, the phone rang beside me. It was Peter's girlfriend, Cynthia, calling from her dormitory at Columbia. Earlier I had asked Isabella to try to reach Cynthia's mother, but I did not know that she had. I had not heard Cynthia's voice before because one of the boys had always answered when she called Peter at Christmas time. She and Peter had met in the summer but only begun to date in November. We talked quite calmly. I gave her only a few details and told her what Peter's note said. "This was my decision," followed by his signature.

"That sounds just like him," she said. We went on to talk about how she might contact Wendy, Peter's apartment mate, and come with her to the service we had planned for Saturday afternoon. Our voices were so even. No tears. I think if she had been less shocked, less affected, Cynthia might have been crying.

That first night, Tom and Carolyn slept in the guest room up under the eaves at the back of the house. They kept a light on all night.

I had slept up there the night before, slipping quietly out of our room when I couldn't sleep and making my way gingerly in the dark, up the creaky, little circular staircase. A book of short stories was on the table so I read for a while, then lay thinking about the projects that Brooks and I were pursuing in our early retirements from teaching. His antiques business had dwindled. I was not sure I could establish myself as a tutor. At least, I thought, the children were each on track. Just as a little light began to creep around the shades, I awoke with tears in my eyes and a gentle, indefinable sadness. I have thought since that it is possible that at the moment of my waking, Peter climbed out onto the stone window ledge of his fourteenth floor room and jumped into a gray mist.

I know now how and where he landed. An article in the Boston University newspaper reported such details. It said someone had called out, "There's a jumper!" I have stood in the street and tried to envision the commotion, a police car coming, night workers looking out, sirens, an ambulance.

We learned from the hotel that Peter had checked in between eight and nine o'clock in the evening and had paid for his room with cash. His belongings had been given over to the police along with his note. There are questions I would now ask. Did he get into the bed? I saw it two years later. It's queen size and takes up much of the small room which narrows away from the window. Was the TV on? He always had it on whenever we took him to hotels and motels. I had pictured the set in a different part of the room. Were the clothes from his sports bag, two or three pairs of underpants, khakis, two shirts, odd socks, strewn all over the place? I had picked up his clothes and Tom's in many of the rooms they shared on our trips. Was the wash case unpacked in the bathroom? He had filled it with all sorts of items with which to make himself presentable for a day of classes, shaving lotion, deodorant, two mouthwashes.

He also packed two textbooks, one on abnormal psychology and one on communications. They were new, stiff, shiny and unmarked; the charges for them would come in on his Visa bill in February along with others for the new term's books and supplies. Inside a spiral notebook was a sheet from his computer containing several short news clips he had written on recent events, Bush's inauguration, new evidence in the Iran-Contra scandal. Peter's college schedule for the term showed that on Wednesdays he had a journalism class, the one in which they were using a new computer program that confused him.

Tom says Peter could hardly get the words out when he tried to talk about his fear of failing with this program. That was Monday evening when Tom called him from school. Tom suggested that he drop the course but Peter said he couldn't because it was part of his major. Tom had called to amuse his brother with a story about a Westminster hockey game but when he got around to telling it he realized that Peter wasn't really listening. Then Tom had to go to rehearsal.

"Something must have happened on Tuesday," Tom says. But we have no idea how Peter spent that day except for his call to me at noon. It didn't occur to me to ask Jeff, Peter's closest friend, or Wendy, until after we had lost contact with both of them. Wendy did tell Carolyn that she knew that something was wrong with Peter on Monday night but that he would not talk about it.

The funeral home we had called is in a white frame house set back a little from the main street of Lenox. On

Thursday morning, in one of its two front rooms, Brooks and I talked to a young man, the son of the owner. He was very kind but clearly uneasy with us. He said that, although it was contrary to their usual advice, it would be better if we did not see Peter. But I knew I must see him, so we agreed that I could come again the next morning.

The closest I would get to Peter that day would be to unpack the bag he had taken to the hotel and go through his wallet, which was handed to us in a brown manilla envelope. I did not choose to open the plastic trash bag containing the clothes Peter wore when he jumped, but I thought I could tell as I touched the thin surface that his old ski jacket was in it, the one he had worn to the hospital on an August night almost two and a half years earlier.

Before we left, Brooks and I went into a room across the center hall and quickly chose the least offensive coffin we could find. I have little recollection of its outside, but the inside was made of a satin-like material. If it is possible for white to be lurid, that is how it looked to me.

In Peter's almost empty drawers I found an old green cotton sweater and in his closet, a frayed yellow shirt I had washed, ironed and hung there after Christmas. He had left no pants that still fit him so I took the khakis from his sports bag, saw that they were quite dirty and put them in the washing machine, then the dryer. Almost as soon as they were dry, the door bell rang and I handed the soft pants with the sweater and shirt and two unmatched white socks to the young man from the funeral home.

I thought later that this young man and his father probably would have been relieved if we had asked to have Peter cremated, but neither Brooks nor I wanted that. It seemed to me that Peter was enough destroyed.

"I thought you shouldn't go alone," Carolyn said. And so, unwisely for her, I think, she came with me on Friday morning. We stood in the room where Brooks and I had sat the day before. Several yards into the room (I remember it as being further away than it possibly could have been) was the coffin. Peter lay propped at an uneasy angle. Only the green of his sweater and his thick brown hair curling on his brow looked familiar. His face was waxen, all the curves and angles not quite right, like a bad portrait.

Behind me, I heard Carolyn's voice rise. "It's Peter, but it's not Peter!" I saw only the blur of her coat as she turned away from me and fell back onto a stiff sofa in the hall.

I looked at Peter for a moment longer and then we left. It was getting colder and there was an icy slush on the ground.

On Saturday afternoon, Tom stood up at the far end of the living room. People were seated on all the chairs, on the sofa, and on the floor. Others stood around the edges and out into the dining area. Many of them were young men, Peter's friends, some of whom I had never met. Tom held a piece of paper on which was a copy of one of the essays he'd written for college applications. It was the one he had been working on the last time he saw his brother, when Peter passed by the living room door on his way to bed the night before New Year's Eve.

Tom started. "When I was growing up, I spent a great deal of time with my older brother." His descriptions of his and Peter's many battles made people laugh a little. Then he spoke of Peter's bout with depression two years earlier, and of his recovery. The essay ended with the words, "I admire my brother." Tom added a few sentences, saying finally to the sea of faces, "I'll always love you, Peter."

I had already read something I had written about Peter's last year and Carolyn had read two letters Peter had written her. Others spoke, my two middle sisters, my mother, and my friend, Ann. But it was Tom that many people remember best, standing tall and thin, his strong, recently-matured features pale, and his brown hair curling along a brow very much like his brother's. (We still call him "Pete" sometimes, and then we hear ourselves and apologize. He always says, "It's okay," and I think how odd are these polite exchanges over a slip that went unnoticed when Peter was alive.)

Everyone milled around for a while after the service. A few people had come some distance. Peter's friends gravitated towards the food Carolyn and Liz had set out.

When I go to Peter's grave now with its headstone in place and the grass plot almost blending with the area around it, I can't imagine how the four of us stood along one side. But that day, the trench, which had been dug for Peter, appeared enormous as did his coffin suspended part way down. We each reached to place a few flowers on it. I don't know where anyone else stood; I had asked only my family and Peter's friends to come with us. As the minister pronounced the familiar farewell, I muttered, "I don't believe in any of this crap." Brooks put a restraining hand on my arm. I thought that Peter would not have been surprised by my behavior.

The minister stopped and the four of us broke ranks. I don't remember speaking to anyone in my family. I know that my father and Isabella's family stayed in their car. But I became aware of Peter's friends, especially Jeff. He stood in a dark coat at the foot of the grave looking down at Peter's coffin. I went to touch his shoulder. He and Peter had been lightning rods for each other's humor. It was Jeff's voice I'd heard most often in recent years asking, "Is Pete there?" And they would go off to play some golf or tennis or take in a movie. "Nothing you'd like, Mom," Peter usually said when I'd ask what they had seen. Jeff and Peter had been at the same party the weekend before. Maybe some of the others had been there too.

"It wasn't sadness I saw in their faces that day," Brooks said to me later. "It was bewilderment."

Cynthia and Wendy, who had driven from Boston, came back to the house with us. It must have been nearly four o'clock by then. The girls sat on the sofa as they had during the service. We talked quite casually for a while. We even laughed as they described the odd looks they had received from a desk clerk at the seedy hotel where they had spent the previous night. Cynthia had not wanted to stay in the apartment where she had stayed with Peter only two weeks before.

Peter had described our house to each of the girls so they wanted a tour. We started in the basement, by then abandoned to leaks and musty storage, where a few years before the children had watched TV and played ping pong and rougher games. I pointed to the gashes in the ceiling where hockey sticks had gone through. From there, we trooped back up the circular iron staircase to the room which currently doubled as TV room and Brooks' office, with its typewriter, copying machine and file cabinet full of records of his antiques business and the local committees on which he served.

On many nights in recent years, I had opened that door on a blaring TV to wave good night at Peter and Tom, sprawled on the carpeting with their backs against two big easy chairs. "Clean up before you leave and shut the cat in," I'd say in futile battle with the TV and trying not to look at the empty soda bottles rolling around, the spilling dorritos bags and the cigarette butts piling up in an ashtray beside Peter. He always promised he was going to stop when he turned twenty-four. Now Tom smokes more than Peter ever did.

I closed the door on the blank TV screen and led Cynthia and Wendy across the living room down the narrow hall to Peter's room and opened his door; it had already become an unspoken rule that it should be closed. The room was dimly lit from the hall and by the fading light in the window facing west, and it was warm because I had turned the heat up earlier to make the room smell as it had when Peter was home. His bed stood in the center near the south window. He had left the bed neat but I had remade it with clean sheets and an extra blanket against a midwinter visit. The bureau loomed high in the far corner. Peter never rearranged his things the way Carolyn and Tom did, so the shapes on his bureau were those which had been there for years; a couple of tall mugs holding loose change from the floor, a painted tray full of trinkets from Christmas stockings and Easter baskets. Across from the bureau, the bookcase full of sports stories was lost in the space where Peter's desk had been before he moved it to Boston.

I must have told the girls that I had recently removed my ironing board and drying rack from the room, because as I closed the door, Cynthia said, "Oh, yes. My mother has started using my room for laundry."

Soon after Cynthia and Wendy left, my mother and my two middle sisters, who do not have families, appeared for dinner. They were staying at an inn in town; my father had gone home with Isabella and her family. That evening, I could still talk to my mother and sisters. After a few weeks, I would recoil from their efforts to console me.

A few days later, one sister called to say she had figured out what had happened to Peter. I did not let her go on. I knew even then that that question would haunt much of the rest of my life. And I had already made an appointment for the four of us with Peter's psychiatrist.

3

A WEEK AND A DAY AFTER PETER'S DEATH, BROOKS, CAROLYN AND I drove to Westminster, picked up Tom, and drove on to McLean Hospital in Belmont, near Boston. Sitting in four chairs, crowded into a room intended only for patient and therapist, we told Dr. Rhodes what we each had seen and heard of Peter in the eleven weeks since his last therapy session. The only person I remember looking at was Tom. He sat in his long dark coat, flushed with fever, coughing, as he recounted his last call to Peter.

Although I was conscious that Dr. Rhodes was handling us carefully, I believed him when he said that he had been so shocked when I had called to tell him of Peter's suicide, that he had felt for a moment that someone must have pushed him. I spoke of the fact that early in January Peter had turned down a dorm room at B.U. for which he had applied in November. When I described how upset Peter was after he made this decision, Dr.Rhodes shook his head and said that he did not think it would have been at all good for Peter to try to live in a dorm. He then assured us several times that there was no way we could have known, nothing we could have done. It was an assurance I would hear from many people:

friends, family and doctors and one which I would not believe.

That night, we stayed in a motel in Brookline near my parents' house. In the dining room, we sat hidden by the high fan-shaped backs of wicker chairs and struggled with the menu. Tom's eyes were not only guarded but gleaming with fever.

By morning, we could see that an icy rain would make the turnpike hazardous. Brooks called and was advised against driving. I could not imagine how we would get through the day—a day in Boston was for having lunch with friends and tea with my mother, for movies and shopping.

Brooks and I sat through some sort of breakfast and took tea and some of the rolls we had ordered up to the children. When Tom came fully awake, he said that he wanted to see Peter's apartment one more time. I wanted to go, too, to find Peter's journals and stories and bring them home.

We made our way to the stretch of Commonwealth Avenue that winds into Allston and stopped at the end of a block of narrow buildings. Brooks said he could not go in and Carolyn decided to stay in the car with him. Tom and I went in, up two flights of stairs and unlocked the door to Number 8 with Peter's key.

Wendy greeted us then went back into her room which was the living room. We went by the little kitchen area and into Peter's small room. I had never been there before but Tom had stayed with his brother in June. The bed, which dominated the room, was covered by a striped sheet I had ordered in the summer. Beside it, on the floor, a book lay face down, a paperback edition of *A Confederacy of Dunces*. I had not read it but I knew the young man who wrote it had committed suicide prior to its publication. Tom picked it up and said, "He'd almost finished it."

Clothing was lying around, but most of it was piled in and on the crates in which Peter kept everything. When I saw his new down ski jacket hanging over the top of the closet door, I knew that what I had felt through the garbage bag at home had to have been his old jacket.

I was going through Peter's desk, looking for the journals, when Tom pulled several crumpled sheets of computer paper from the wastebasket. We held them to the light and read hurriedly. Each page began the same way with a line at the top which read, "I had Professor Banks for News Writing and Reporting I." Then came Peter's name and below that the dateline, "Kingston, Jamaica," followed by a two-line paragraph. "Peter Brooks Butler of Allston, a twenty-two-year-old student, died aboard the cruise ship, Sea Mist, from food poisoning on January 18th at 4 p.m."

I realized that Peter had been assigned to write his own obituary, just what I had heard Brooks tell him he might be asked to do, when they were talking at Christmas time about the upcoming term. Brooks had had to do the same years before in a journalism course.

Peter continued with information about his life, in some versions adding inappropriate details like how he cut his head in a fall when he was four. Near the end of each version, he started a paragraph, "Mr. Butler leaves behind..." and listed the four of us, followed always by the line, "Of his brother's demise," Thomas said, "I'm devastated. I've lost more than a brother. I've lost my best friend."

We didn't say much as I flattened the pages out and slipped them into one of the accordion file folders I had found in a drawer of the desk along with the brown plastic notebooks I recognized as Peter's journals. As I pocketed the folded Boston University newspaper Wendy had left on the desk, I caught sight only of the headline, "Comm School Student Suicide." Carolyn had made Wendy read the article to her over the phone to make sure it didn't imply that Peter's death had anything to do with alcohol or drugs because, as she said, "That wasn't Peter."

Back at the motel, Carolyn and I found, at the end of one of the notebooks, some typed pages with dates for the month just passed, January 1989. He had started, "Whether this will turn in to a serious personal journal, I don't yet know. I think

I'm going to play it by ear." Peter had not used those words for his writing before so we sat down on the bed and read as quickly as we could, expectantly, as though he would tell us something we could not have known. But it was familiar territory.

January 1, 1989: I woke up today dismayed to recall that I had promised myself last night that I would go jogging as soon as I got up. Only the thought of taking a half-time break in my run by stopping off at work enabled me to actually get myself on the road.

I was done with the run by 11:30 A.M. A lot of free time was ahead of me and what I dread most about my life in Boston was staring me in the face—loneliness. I was fresh from a week at home. Home is not an exciting place. In fact, it's not really even my home anymore. But at my parents' house, I'm hardly ever alone.

I've spent a lot of solitary hours at 1381 Commonwealth Avenue, so it's not like I'm not used to it. But today my emotional system just was not going to put up with sitting alone in front of the tv set. It wasn't that I felt I couldn't take it. It was just like a part of my system was not going to put up with it. I guess it was kind of like when your stomach just says enough to the shit you've been shoveling down, and decides to send it all back up again.

Anything not to fall into that chair in front of the TV set.

I called John. He had gone to Buffalo to see the play-off game. I called Aldie. No answer. I was getting depressed but at least I could take consolation in the fact that I called. If I'm lonely and I'm too chicken shit to even do something about it, then I really get down. I also called Cynthia. She was home but I wasn't asking her to come over. Instead, I was telling her that there was a chance I might not be able to come down to New York next weekend. It hurt me to hear how disappointed she was, but it also felt good that she cared so much. Thoughts of her have become my "white noise" lately.

I ended up having Sunday lunch with Nana and Papa. Going to that house in Brookline is always an escape, but as a last resort from fending off being by myself, it ain't too bad. And besides, I get free eats.

Still not ready for an empty apartment, I went over to my sister's after I left Nana and Papa. She wasn't up to much so I suc-

ceeded in persuading her to go to a movie.

I don't know what today's feelings portend for the future. Will I gradually just get used to being alone much of the time? I will. Will I wade through the chicken shit and meet more people and do more things? At the very least, I will not let myself settle for anything less than a combination of the two.

So what is the featured obstacle for tomorrow? I will call Mr. Pincus at his office to issue a challenge to his fifth spot on the squash ladder. A challenge. Just thinking about it makes me feel like an asshole. Will I be an asshole for doing it? No. Can I call him up and specifically ask for a challenge? Yes. Will I? yes.

He was restless that night, Carolyn said, and excited over his date with Cynthia the night before.

Later, he told Brooks he did challenge Mr. Pincus and won. That victory put Peter on the club team but he added characteristically that he was sure he'd be off it before they even had a match.

January 4: Today my typewriter is in better shape, and so am I. I started out the day strongly by making myself write a newspaper article. Having done that, no matter what else I do the rest of the day, it will not be a total loss.

I'm finding little, if any, satisfaction in recounting the day's events. Suffice to say it was really fucking cold, and now I'll get on to what is really bothering me at the moment.

I tried to get a hold of Cynthia when I got home this evening, just to talk and set up some preliminary plans for the weekend. Well, every time I tried to get through to her, all I got was this canned voice telling me I had reached the phone mail service. Now I know that Columbia is changing its phone service, but what the hell is the phone mail service?It sounds so damn impersonal. I guess the system is so modern that it has its own "in house" answering service. At least, that's what I'm hoping is the case. Otherwise, something might be wrong with Cynthia's phone line and maybe because of this malfunction, I won't be able to visit her in New York City this weekend. Of course, on the other hand, you dumb fuck, maybe you'll find out something from housing tomorrow that will make it in your own best interest to stay here for the weekend.

Okay, Pete, with or without Cynthia, you are going to get that resume out to the Entertainment Network and you are going to go to Boston University Housing.

The next page was not typed and contained only a short paragraph, Peter's cramped angular letters conveying more of his distress than the words themselves.

January 5: If I want to live in a newly designated Boston University quarters, I will have to pay rent on my apartment while I'm living on campus. Is it worth it? I can afford to do it. Can I afford not to do it?

If you're gonna do it, you can't make trap doors.

Peter and I had talked on the phone that day and decided that he could afford to pay his share of the apartment for a month, or even two, to give Wendy time to find another roommate. My father, who had been paying his board for the academic year, could pay for the dorm room instead. Brooks who was listening to my end of the conversation suggested that Peter should try to make contact with his prospective roommate. I passed that on and Peter agreed to try to call him. At the time I was more worried about Peter's health as his voice was heavy with bronchitis.

The next day he planned to escape his small apartment and recuperate at my parents house. But when he arrived in the late afternoon my mother was out and my father on hearing Peter cough sent him away for fear of contagion. Peter walked the short distance to his sister's apartment where she gave him something to eat and tried to make him comfortable before she went out.

Carolyn said, "I knew he was feeling bad, Mom, I almost didn't go out that Friday."

Peter and I had talked about the dorm room again that night. He had discovered that his prospective roommate was traveling. I wanted him to consider whether he really wanted to share a room again. I could well have used the phrase "total stramger."

January 7: Needless to say, when I woke up this morning in my sister's apartment, I didn't feel much like attacking the world.

I didn't begin to feel much better until I decided I wasn't going to take the apartment on campus. I basically didn't take it because I just couldn't get myself to risk moving into the same bedroom with a total stranger. That doesn't seem too unreasonable to me except it leaves me in the same social situation that drove me to consider moving out in the first place. The "which" isn't the worst fate in the world. The problem is right now I feel bowled over by my whole being. Part of me is not reacting like I made a reasonable decision in not moving on campus. Instead, I'm feeling like I did two years ago when I left Ithaca College after only five days and Mom and Dad took me to the hospital. I mean, fuck, right this minute my face is physically tingling. It's fucking scary. I mean, hell, it's not like I goddamn threw everything away just because I decided I didn't want to move into the same room with a total stranger. But tell my body that. That period of escape combined with my decision that I couldn't deal with the risk involved in moving in with a total stranger has really thrown me for a loop.

Well, I'm gonna fight it because this is my life and I gotta do something, like some sit-ups now. I'll check in tomorrow.

Peter had written of his attack in some of the same words he would use to me on the phone the following evening. "My face was tingling, Mom. The whole bit. Like the night you took me to the emergency room."

At first I had had a sensation of something dropping within me but somehow incredibly I had rallied even as we talked. The night he referred to was more than two years earlier. This time he had not collapsed. He had had an anxiety attack and gotten himself through it. I could hear myself explaining this to a friend who had known of Peter's troubles, making it sound encouraging.

January 10: The last time I checked in I was pretty fucked up. I don't know as I'm any less fucked up this time, but at least my face isn't vibrating with anxiety. Why it's not, as it was when I made my last entry, I'm not sure. Maybe because my decision not to move on campus is more final now. Actually, not more final. It is final. So with that done am I now just sliding back into the same old routine that brought me to the point where I wanted to leave this apartment? Probably I am doing that, to some extent, which is a depressing realization but a liveable one if I can bring myself to take the opportunities to change other aspects of my life, for example, doing inter-mural sports, getting a summer internship, getting onto the squash ladder, etc. When I was really wigging out a couple of days ago, I would think of these things and others as well, and it would make me feel better. But why did it make me feel better? Because I knew these were things I was going to do that would help to change the rhythm of my life? No, unfortunately, that's not the reason. It's almost like I thought these projects were going to happen to me and I would somehow be transported from my less than perfect existence. God knows I've experienced this kind of dynamic before, and I've certainly been burned by it before, but that didn't prevent my psyche from falling back on it for support. Anything to ease the pain. Well, the pain is subsiding now, and it's time for me to tackle what these projects really portend at least initially, fear, anxiety, and you at home can choose a third.

Brooks and I had gone to Boston for a couple of nights that week. The first afternoon I had been out shopping when Peter called my mother's house. If I had been there he would have stopped by on his way to work. The next day, as planned, he had had lunch with Brooks while I visited my sister, Isabella. Peter told his father that Cynthia, who was due to spend the weekend with her family in Wellesley, was coming from New York a day early to see him. She had not stayed a night in Peter's apartment before. So when Brooks told me of this plan I had seen it as a step forward in their relationship, one which I thought Peter would welcome.

January 13: Should I even be writing about Cynthia? I mean, literally, she's such a small part of my life and it's very important that I don't let the emptiness of my life here in Boston drive me into thinking that what I have with Cynthia is anything that extends past the next phone call or the next visit.Cynthia and thoughts connected to her sometimes get used as escape routes to a comfort zone when my existence looks particularly bleak. But I guess as long as I at least recognize that the thought pattern is one in the service of escape, then, hopefully, I won't get into too much trouble.

I mean if I start planning my summer and if placing Cynthia in Boston becomes a main attraction to it, then I'm setting myself up for a big fall if she goes elsewhere, or dies instead, or whatever.

It was that type of attitude I was trying to keep in touch with over the past twenty-four hours I spent with Cynthia. Did I think about it too much? I mean, to the extent that I couldn't even enjoy the moment with her? Heck, even if I could see her every day, I would still be down in the dumps about the rest of my life, except I probably wouldn't be as driven, if you can call it that, to change my life. So right now, it's just as well that Cynthia is in New York every day and not in my apartment though there are some therapeutic aspects about being around her.

The fact is that her life seems to have many things that I wish mine did, or at least, I think I wish it did. Now when you're in a relationship with somebody like this, there are two basic ways it can go. One, you can live vicariously through your mate's achievements, or two, you can be jealous as hell of them and, consequently, have a misdirected hostile surge rankle your innards whenever you see this person. I've felt both ways toward Cynthia but I know that I will be best off if I remember that she has hacked her way through a lot of the stuff that I will have to go through, so there is no point or validity in idealizing her existence. It's just a waste of time that would be better spent trying to get yourself through some of the "Stuff."

Peter's injunction to himself sounded so mild, so normal, so possible. If I had read the journal the week before I don't think I would have realized that he was in danger. Only later would I come to hear the alarm in some of his phrases.

Carolyn said that the last time she and Peter had lunch together he told her he wasn't sure how to manage his relationship with Cynthia because she was in New York.

We flipped back and forth to see if there was any later entry. There wasn't. Classes had started three days later and Peter must have begun to work on the obituary assignment.

A little later, as the four of us walked in a light, icy mist towards Carolyn's apartment, I saw a trash can and threw the BU paper into it. I didn't want Tom to see it.

The familiar warmth of the apartment was a relief. Tom and I talked to Liz while Carolyn and Brooks went off to buy sandwiches. After we ate, Tom fell asleep on the couch. Carolyn said she and Tom would stay the extra night there.

On the strength of my relief that the day was passing, I decided to walk to my mother's house to return an umbrella I had borrowed the day before. My route across the bridge, down the hill and up again was a reversal of Peter's just three weeks earlier on the day my father did not want to catch his cold. I pictured him, his shoulders hunched, going for the last time, down the wide steps and out through the brick pillars at the end of the driveway. I refused tea as I had on the previous day. I could not even sit down in that living room where I had sat a few weeks earlier on the afternoon when I had shopped too late to see Peter. My father appeared on the staircase and said, "Are you feeling better today?"

For once, my mother snapped at him. "Of course she's not." Yet by spring, she would be begging me to do just that, to feel better, saying in desperation, "Other people lose more than one child." We never talked of my father's feelings about Peter, because I suspect that he never said much to her about him. I did not want to ask because she had always attributed feelings to him that he never expressed. It was hard to have a conversation with him. His question, "Are you asking me or telling me?" rang through our childhoods and did not stop as we grew up. We were always meant to be asking. He did all the telling.

Right after Peter's funeral service, my father had come up to me as I walked out of the living room. He didn't touch me, but said, "I want you to know I've cancelled Peter's rent check." I did not react. His concern was a familiar one; he didn't want the wrong person to get his money. A few minutes later, he said the same thing to Brooks. It was the only remark he addressed to either of us that day.

I came to feel that my father had cancelled Peter along

with the check, like the bad investment he had turned out to be. A few years earlier, my mother had persuaded my father that they should pay for the educations of their six grandchildren. When my father passed this decision on to me, he said, "Your mother and I will make sacrifices if necessary." I thanked him. I knew enough about the assets he had garnered from the seed money of my mother's inheritance to be sure they would not have to make any sacrifices.

At that time my father was nearly eighty and my mother hoped he would set up a fund from which the children could draw their school expenses. But he did not acquiesce to that. He continued to handle the purse strings. As Peter often observed, "Papa thinks he's immortal."

That afternoon, my father, seeing that I was not going to settle down for tea and behave as he thought I should, retreated up the stairs. I left my mother standing forlorn and bent in the dim wide hall. I did not yet know that I would not be able to make myself go back to that house again.

When Brooks and I were alone at the motel in the evening the time passed a little more easily than it had the night before. The next day, the four of us drove home. In the past, as we had returned from trips, I had always liked to catch sight of the dark red boards of our house across the fields, to assure myself that it stood unharmed. When the five of us were in the car, we would burst out of it in relief, Brooks and I exhorting the children to carry in their belongings as they quickly melted into their favorite places in the house. That morning, the house looked wet and stark, unwelcoming. Once inside, it took me a long time to gather it around me again, to turn it back into our house, to look into Peter's room and turn up the heat.

Before dinner while Brooks was warming up something for us to eat—not his usual job—I took one of the yellow spiral notebooks Susan had given me the week before and went up to the guest room. She is an artist, but she seemed to know that I would need to write. I started, "It has been ten days since Peter died. I do not know if writing it down will do me good or harm. Peter was a big boy and I loved his bigness. Tall and thin at times—chunky as a little boy. Strong and filled out and proud of his strength before he took his life away…"

4

"THE WORLD LOOKS MORE LIKE JANUARY THAN IT DID WHEN PETER died," I wrote in my journal on a Saturday afternoon. It snowed more on that first day of April than it had through all the winter. Brooks came down to our room from the guest room where he had gone to read and doze. I was in my chair half watching an old movie, my arms wound around my legs to keep my whole body from shaking, a position that had come to frighten him. He sat on the edge of his bed, pulling on and slowly tying his heavy leather boots and said, "I realized, when I woke up just now, that we would never be happy again."

I nodded and said, "Yes," feeling as though I had known that for a long time.

A little later I wandered up the street for an hour taking the opposite direction from my morning walk. As I came back towards our driveway I saw Brooks go off across the fields through the layer of wet snow.

In the living room I sat in the chair where I had sat nine weeks before during the service for Peter. We had recently had that room added with the idea of entertaining more as the children left home. I could not imagine that it would ever be full of people again. Brooks returned with pussy willows he had cut, went to town to buy jonquils and combined them in two vases on either side of the room. I heard him say to himself, "At least they look pretty." They made me cry because there was no one to see them but me and I could not enjoy them.

At dinner we passed the hand phone back and forth as we talked to each of the children. They called almost every evening, Carolyn first, usually. "It's me," her voice faded apologetically as though she knew she had nothing to tell us that we wanted to hear. Yet she had no one else in whom she dared confide her vivid nightmares of Peter in pain and her own terror that she might someday be like him and be driven to kill herself even though she had never thought of such a thing before. She sensed that no one understood why she hadn't been able to return to the chaos of her job at Quincy Market or a room full of daycare children. "They just don't get it." She would say her voice now rising in anguish and frustration.

Sometimes the phone rang as she hung up and it was Tom, but often he called much later. He was no longer living on any sort of boarding school schedule; he could neither get to sleep nor wake up on time. He was missing classes and tests and struggling over papers he could never seem to finish. He had raised alarms about his academic work before but had ended up on the high honors list every term for three and a half years. That spring he was on the middle list. "Ironic, Mom, just where Peter always was." One night he said he thought he must be getting less selfish because he realized that he would be willing to flunk out of Westminster and not get into any college if he could have Peter back.

When people said, as they often did, "But you still have two children," I realized that they could have no concept of such conversations.

When the brief April snows melted Brooks began to rake the dried grass and pull the hay off his flower beds. Over fifteen years he had created a lovely place from a cow pasture, but now he told me he was just working out of habit, that it seemed pointless.

He wasn't sure he should leave me alone for a night but I assured him he could and he went a few times to stay at my parents' house and look for a small apartment as we had planned to do just before Peter died.

On those spring evenings when I was alone, I lay on my bed and watched the soft light fade on the mountain. I was conscious of the frame of the house around me and of the sounds that separated themselves from the swirling blood in my ears, the racing tick of the little gold carriage clock on the mantle, or the ghost-child creak of the cat as she made her way up the stairs to one of the guest room beds. The hours passed more easily then than during the day. It didn't matter if I cried, or bothered to eat or even moved. I could let my mind slip.

As the evening freight train passed on tracks that ran between the woods and the mountain, its whistle seemed to call from over the hill where Peter was buried. Its sound could carry me out the window all the way across town to a hillside on its west and the house from which Peter was born.

The time was so short, only an hour and a half, between my waking in pain on a November night and Peter's birth in a hospital six miles away, that it always seemed as if he was born *from* the house. Two-year-old Carolyn made the night car trip with us, standing behind my seat in her floppy-footed pajamas, holding my shoulder and saying over and over, "It's all right, Mummy."

The house of Peter's babyhood was built just below a curve in the long, dark drive of pine trees leading to the big H-shaped, stucco house where my grandmother spent her summers. Her house had been the magic place of my childhood, its winter landscape unknown to me then except in the pictures of the early years of my grandmother's marriage and my mother's childhood.

The pattern of our days in those summer visits didn't vary much. Right after lunch, my grandmother would retreat to her room for a nap while the other adults either did the same or read the newspapers in the living room. The younger children, two of my sisters and my cousins, were bedded down on the third floor and my sister Julia and I were free to wander or choose a book from the cases in the wide, green-carpeted hall and read in our rooms over the front door.

In my teens I chose romantic stories and sat reading in a high backed chair by the window. After a while I would rest my head against the brown cotton slip cover, and listen to the sway of the high pines along the driveway as I imagined a future romance of my own.

For many years even as an adult, I would find my grandmother's house a place of refuge and of dreams. So it always seemed incredible that Brooks drove up her driveway one early autumn Saturday when I was twenty-eight. He was a teacher in a boys' boarding school in the town of Lenox and had been invited to lunch by my aunt, my mother's older sister. She was the family matchmaker—she had introduced my parents to each other—and she had suffered an unrequited love for Brooks' uncle when she was about eighteen.

My aunt was determined. The following fall, she issued another invitation to Brooks and after that, he and I began to pay attention to each other.

About two years after the second introduction, we were married, and two years after that, at the time of Carolyn's birth, we started to build our house below my grandmother's, on land which she had given us. The long unused meadow was surrounded by pines punctuated with stands of birches except on one side where, from the French doors of our living room, we looked out on the same blue-green hills I had always seen from my grandmother's terrace. Even in winter, when I was alone with two small children and any outing meant so much bundling and uphill pushing, I could look out the windows and feel that I didn't want to live anywhere else.

I had a remarkably agile seventy-nine-year-old babysitter at that time. But Peter did not challenge her mobility. At almost two, he was satisfied to sit on the floor while she ironed and when I returned, she would smile at him indulgently, point to his head and say, "It's all up there with that one." Whatever Peter had conveyed to Mrs. Gainey, in the handful of words then at his disposal, had convinced her that he was going to be a thinker rather than a runner.

I watch children now and mentally divide them into Peters and non-Peters, the latter being those who move like motors, all of a piece. Peter's body took its commands one at a time and in the beginning very slowly. He mastered his spoon and some elementary conversation before he got his feet going. When, at two, he grew too big to be carried, I was always pulling him along and hoisting him into his carriage or the car. He seldom made a fuss and his reaction to tones of disapproval or raised voices was to go to the nearest wall and turn his back on the speakers.

Peter's earliest memory came from that third year of his life, the last we spent in the house of his babyhood. "Were the door handles black with latches that lifted?" He asked me years later when he showed me the piece he had written about that memory.

It was entitled *First Lie.*

> *I'm two years old, maybe two and a half. It is early morning and my bedroom looks damp and gray but it is probably warm enough.*
>
> *I'm awake earlier than usual and clutching hopefully the top of my crib. My hands are too small to get a firm grip. Where is Mom? I'm up. Why isn't she? I can't hold on forever; I've got to do something and quickly.*
>
> *Early morning is a difficult time for many people to form thoughts. The brain is littered with a variety of residual notions. Fortunately, due to my age, I don't have this problem. Most of my thoughts serve the moment at hand and then are allowed to drift away when a new need arises. Anyway, Mom will want to know I'm up.*

I think for a short time as my sweaty little fingers start to ache. I decide to cough. I feel fine aside from the ache which has now reached my forearms, but that's got nothing to do with coughing. My mother does not sleep deeply; she will hear me cough.

My cough is hollow and scrapes awkwardly off my dry throat. I manage three or four hacks and then stop to listen. I have no idea what patience is. My thirst for attention has become more important than the pain which has now snuck up my arms and wrapped itself around my shoulders.

My eyes, now clouded with the beginnings of tears, are fixed on the black latch of my bedroom door. I do not retain a great deal, but I know that when that latch goes up, I get to come out.

Nothing is happening. I feel a pit of anger taking root in my stomach. I'm going to cough again. My mother will come in. I don't care. I'm a bitter little boy.

I start to cough again but stop abruptly at the sound of groaning bed springs. I strain my ears. Two ropes of pain have now met and tied a knot in the middle of my neck. My parents are talking tiredly to each other. Should I cough again? Even at two, you have a sense about going to the well too many times.

More bed springs ache out loud. Maybe my father is coming to get me. That would be all right, except his bony hands hurt my sides. The floor in my parent's room is creaking under steps. They are my mother's steps. When you rely on other people to get you out of bed, you learn to recognize footsteps A latch snaps up, the one on my parent's door. I want to let go of the railing and rest my head on the back of my stuffed bear. I don't dare though; my mother might think I've gone back to sleep. And I could never produce a serious cough from the prone position.

The warped floor bows away from the bottom of the door, allowing me to see the tops of my mother's slippers. The latch lifts as I rest my head against the railing. The door swings open silently. My mother pads in softly, followed by a rich smelling draught. I raise my head just as my mother is lowering hers. My eyes see a nourishing smile, and I feel a hand snaking around my head and settling to tickle the back of my neck. She wants to know what all this coughing is about as she places a warm hand on my cool forehead.

These images, which delighted me when I first read

them, have come to haunt me as I wonder what I could have done for Peter in his earliest years to make him less hesitant to ask for help.

Our idyll on my grandmother's hill lasted barely five years. She had died soon after Peter was born and two years later, her property was sold to a man who intended to build houses all around ours. Soon after the sale took place I gave birth to my third child.

Carolyn and Peter were staying with my parents. The baby had not come early as my other two had, so soon after the due date my doctor induced labor. He knew right away that something was wrong with the little girl we named Julie, but neither he nor the pediatrician were able to explain her low birth weight and her inability to suck. She was put in an incubator and as I was only able to peer at her as she lay among the tubes, I was sent home after two days. A few days later Carolyn and Peter were brought back to us. I remember waking each day and thinking how incredible it was not to know if I had three children or still just two.

When no diagnosis or prognosis was forthcoming from the pediatrician, we had Julie transferred to Children's Hospital in Boston in the fourth week of her life. We followed the ambulance and, at the hospital, were told within an hour that she had a genetic abnormality and would live no more than a few months. We arranged to have her placed in a nursing home for terminally ill children located near Lenox.

I don't remember when I first saw the town cemetery to which I now walk frequently, but that summer when we learned that Julie was going to die, we bought a plot at the top of a long gentle slope. There Brooks and I met a minister of our acquaintance on a Saturday in late July. The funeral parlor brought a little white casket that looked like a picnic container. I could only imagine the wraith of a baby I had never even held, whom I could not believe had ever been a part of me.

One hot afternoon a few weeks after we buried Julie, I put Peter in his stroller. He was quiet and compliant as I went down our driveway and up the road to a curve where tourists often stop to look at the red barns centered in the pasture land of the valley. There the road dips sharply and, and as we started down, sobs pulled my shoulders up and shook down through my arms to the hands that held onto the stroller and kept it from careening down the hill. Peter did not turn around, so I could see only the silky, brown hair at the back of his head. I remember wondering what he could sense.

However, it was Carolyn's reaction that Brooks and I were most concerned about that summer. She was five, old enough to have consciously prepared for a new baby and for a few weeks had believed that she had a sister.

The death of the baby and the threat of dire changes in the land around our house led Brooks to follow up on a job opening at a private high school in a town north of Boston. By the time he was offered the job, I had been told there was no reason I couldn't have another child. But I wanted to do so under the care of the Boston doctor to whom a friend had referred me.

It was a hectic autumn. We moved twice, first into a rented house. Brooks was preparing new courses and Carolyn, somewhat reluctantly, was starting kindergarten. In November, we drove the children to Lenox for a last weekend on our hill. The house had been sold and we were going to pack it for movers who would take everything to our newly purchased house in Hamilton.

Our new abode was on a street surrounded by other comfortable, medium-sized houses near the center of town, too near Brooks and I thought, when we could hear the musak from the supermarket. We were not accustomed to a "neighborhood," but Carolyn and Peter happily became part of a small group of children of which Peter was the youngest.

When I reread the obituaries Tom and I had found in Peter's waste basket, I realized that most of the memories he included harked back to the three years we spent in Hamilton. In one, he wrote, "He fell and hit his head on a bathtub and had to get ten stitches."

The injury that required stitches occurred on an autumn Saturday when Peter was almost four, tall for his age but still solid of build. He had been playing with Eric, a wiry, hyperactive seven-year-old boy who lived next door. I was upstairs resting because I was six months pregnant with Tom and a little bleeding had taken me off my feet. There were shrieks from outside, then Brooks calling me in the tight, imperative tone I had come to know meant trouble. I came down to the kitchen to see Peter in his father's arms, blood seeping into his thick hair and down the back of his blue-striped t-shirt. My father was at our house and, with Brooks holding Peter, they drove to the nearest hospital.

When they returned a couple of hours later, the tears were dry on Peter's face and I was shown the neat stitches on the back of his head where a little white space had been cleared in his brown hair. Brooks said Peter had let the doctor work on him without a fuss. Eric was hopping around, anxiously telling us that Peter had tripped, fallen backwards and hit his head on a discarded bathtub. We guessed that Eric had probably pushed him. Peter seemed unsure about what had happened. The wound healed quickly and soon the only reminder of the accident was a faded circle of blood stain on the collar of the t-shirt.

Tom was born that January in Boston. An operation for varicose veins kept me in the hospital for a full week after his birth. On the day Brooks brought Tom and me home, Peter was standing in the kitchen, as we came in from the snow and cold. I lowered the bundled baby towards him and uncovered his face. "You were so red," Peter often told Tom of their first meeting.

I don't remember worrying that winter about how Tom's arrival was affecting Peter. He and Carolyn went on with their games, squabbled no more than usual and sometimes took an interest in their baby brother, she more than he. When

I went for a conference with Peter's nursery school teacher, she told me what a nice child he was, more aware of other people, she said, than most children his age.

In the spring, Eric began to wander into our yard again to play with Peter. He was an only child whose mother had left her husband and son, and he was not usually part of the group our children played with. When we asked Peter about broken windows in a shed behind the garage, he described how Eric had thrown rocks at the windows and added that Eric had also used the shed as a bathroom on occasion and encouraged Peter to do the same. After that, we discouraged Eric from coming over, saying something to the effect that Peter was too young for him. Peter did not object, and it did not occur to me or to Brooks to ask him any more questions about Eric's behavior.

Years later Peter would report to a psychiatrist in some detail about the sex play in which a boy a little older than he had engaged him when he was four or five, adding that he knew that those memories related to some of the fears which had assailed him when he first went to college, fears of being invited by other boys to have oral sex.

For a month that summer, as we had the previous year, we rented an old farmhouse in Lenox. It was on the opposite side of the town from my grandmother's hill and was surrounded by the overgrown pastures of what had been a dairy farm. The children played in the high grass, ran in and out of the red farm sheds and swung on a swing hung from high in an enormous maple. During our third year in Hamilton, the owner of the farm agreed to sell us an eight acre parcel of his fields on the condition that we plan to live on it.

Brooks applied to the day school in Lenox where he had taught before we left and was welcomed back to teach as well as to assist the headmaster. In addition, I would have a chance to get back into the classroom as a part-time history teacher. Carolyn could enter the school's third grade and Peter, a mixed group of kindergarten and first grade known as the Primary. Peter was among the youngest in his kindergarten class in Hamilton and his teacher was hesitant about sending him on to first grade. The Primary seemed a good solution; we could wait and see if he needed another year.

Among Peter's report cards I found a description of him written by his Primary teacher the following March.

> Peter was totally overwhelmed and bewildered by school when he arrived and really did not feel at ease until December when he slowly began to relax and make friends.
>
> He is a thoughtful boy who has very little confidence in himself and avoids risking failure...He asks astute and probing questions which show a range and depth of thinking far beyond what one would expect of a child his age...Peter is a big boy and learning to cope with his physical self requires concentration and effort...another year in Primary is indicated for him.

Most of the boys with whom Peter had begun to play and exchange visits were almost exactly his age, so we thought he had been saved any sense of failure about spending a second year in Primary.

In one version of his obituary assignment, Peter reported our return to Lenox following on his account of his injury. As though old hurts of all kinds were coming back to him he wrote, "Mr. Butler was very disappointed to have to repeat kindergarten."

In my journal I went back to Peter at six. "Could I have changed everything for Peter in those years by paying more attention to him? Was that the whole story? It doesn't seem possible that it could be? It almost seems as if I needed to have had a whole different temperament to make him feel differently about himself."

When I was alone in the house I would get off my bed and go to the photograph albums, the slides and films. Brooks had captured one of the best sequences when Peter was six and Tom two. Clad only in a pair of pajama bottoms, totally relaxed, Peter puts his foot first on one end of the red go-car in which Tom is sitting and then on the other, tipping his brother forward and back, all the while gesturing like a silent movie comic and pulling a baseball cap down over Tom's delighted face.

Such sights of Peter enlarged on the living room shade were my ultimate indulgence. I turned off the projector, rationing the reels and boxes.

5

Brooks and I rarely went up to the graveyard together, but in the late spring we went to measure tombstones and decide what shape and size we wanted for Peter. A long rectangle of new light green grass clearly marked where he lay, the image of it staying in my mind long after we drove away.

At home on a high shelf in the kitchen lay an unopened envelope containing the report of the autopsy done on Peter's body. Neither Brooks nor I wanted to look at it, but we decided we should find a doctor to read it just in case there was something unrelated to Peter's fall that we should know. (Eventually we would learn from a pathologist that there wasn't.) Our first thought was for Brooks to call Jeff's father, who had been Peter's regular doctor, for a reference. I knew he must have said he could not help us, when I heard Brooks shift his voice and ask politely about Jeff's graduation from B.U. Brooks could accommodate everyone, even more than he had before Peter died. I could accommodate no one, not even total strangers.

Sometime that spring I had made myself go to a Price Chopper (not our usual one) for the first time since January and when I arrived at the checkout counter shaking and crying, the young clerk looked right at me as she handed me my change and said, "Have a nice day." I started to scream; banging my cart against the swinging doors, I screamed all the way to my car. By the time a policeman reached me I was in the car and pulling away fast yelling back at him that I didn't give a shit if I had disturbed a few seconds of someone's peace.

The scene wasn't entirely out of character. I had often used swear words in public when I was frustrated or annoyed, even when I knew that I embarrassed Brooks and the children, but I had never before come anywhere near to attracting the attention of a policeman.

I could not tell when these attacks would come and they defied my careful spacing of the tranquilizers designed to control them. The desperation came out more gently in my journals. "There is never a moment of relaxation or forgetting. I cannot get back to myself in body or in mind. I do not know the person I live in."

I looked in the mirror and was surprised at the sameness of my face. My hair, however, had begun to show more white, as I had not rinsed it since Peter's death. I decided to color it brown just one more time for Tom's graduation from Westminster in early June. I pictured myself at the familiar rituals and decided I should look as much as possible like the mother Tom had known for most of his four years at the school.

The weather became bright and warm as graduation weekend approached and I walked in the late afternoons, with an increasing sense that I moved unseen through a technicolor film of blues and greens. On the playing fields of the school down our road children were bright blurs, their voices high-pitched but indistinct. Mothers in cars crossed my path into the parking lot, picked up their children and drove away.

Peter at twelve or thirteen, clad just as those children were, in a long sports jersey, had run full tilt along that sidewalk towards home. The day school bus left him off at the corner half a mile away and he ran because he feared reprisals from some of the boys with whom he had spent his third grade year, boys who now attended the Junior High school he had to pass. He had never been beaten up but some of the tougher kids had made an indelible impression on him.

"There are kids in this town who are out to get me," he would say after he returned to the day school.

As I walked I strung these memories like beads in my mind as though they would lead me inexorably to an understanding of the fears which would assail Peter as a college student. But even then I could see that his early fears had been too ordinary. Some kids are bullies, others their real or imagined victims. Peter's life could be too easily distorted by the reflected light of his death.

I do, however, connect Peter's nightmares with the year he spent in public school, although I know they started earlier. We would hear him cry, a deep, desperate sound and would get him up, sit him on the sofa and struggle to wake him. When we were certain he was awake, we'd put him back to bed, but often the sobs started again and we had to repeat the whole process. The next morning he would come into our room and settle into a comfortable position in bed beside me, seeming unrelated to the child who had cried in the night. He remembered nothing of his nightmares. However, the final paragraph of a description he wrote years later sounds a note of regret about growing out of such morning rituals.

> "...eventually you grow away from the world above the bed and she doesn't tell you to come in when you knock. Instead, you wait and hear feet slap the floor and a hamper or a drawer fly open and slam shut. This is not so bad, because even sooner than you think will come the time when you only see her in the kitchen."

For his fourth grade year Peter returned to the day school where Brooks was then headmaster, having been tapped to help stem the crisis in enrollment. Peter was happy to be back. For the next five years, his teachers often lamented his lack of attention to detail in math and languages but were impressed by his use of words, his questions and comments in class. As one of them put it, "He thinks way beyond the literal."

Such a remark might describe a bookish child, but Peter was a TV child and when he did read, he was not interested in tales of fantasy or even adventure. All his heroes were athletes.

The Christmas he was eight, an elderly aunt sent Peter a book called *Baseball Lore* and for years he read and reread the stories of boys coming from behind to sandlot victories. Soon copies of "Sports Illustrated" cascaded from the cupboard beside his bed and his bookcase filled with picture histories and official encyclopedias of baseball, football, hockey and soccer. When he had absorbed these tomes, Peter engaged his friends and eventually Tom in quizzes about records and averages and even personal details of athletes lives. In these verbal contests, he was unbeatable.

But the blue ribbon on field day and the name read out in assembly were not to be Peter's; it was easy to see why when we went to watch him play soccer or hockey. He stood amidst the fray like a spectator, watching as he figured what should happen next, usually arriving too late to hit or kick. However, on the rare occasion when he found himself in front of the goal with ball or puck at his command, his deliberate shot was strong and straight.

As Peter moved toward his teens, Brooks hoped to broaden his son's interests to include some that had filled his own boyhood like stamp and rock collecting, card and board games. Peter didn't resist these efforts. He just let them slide and returned to his athletes, designing stadiums on shirt cardboards from the laundry. The capacity of any arena was of great interest to him. "How many people do you think this place holds?" he would ask as the five of us settled into theatre seats and, once, as we sat in a church waiting for a bride to appear.

Peter did, however, absorb a good many news items when he flipped through the newspaper and flicked around the TV dial for reports of his favorite teams. And as he read or listened, he began to keep a weather eye out for challenges he sensed would come his way, challenges beyond his world of home and school. He looked up from a Newsweek article when he was about eleven and asked, "What will I do if kids try to make me take dope someday?" I made the trite comment about saying 'no', but he was not convinced. One day as we passed a garage Peter looked in at the young men working on a car. He had never had any desire to do anything mechanical, but he asked me if he would have to go to college to get a job like that. I assured him that going to college would be his decision to make six or seven years hence. Then he wanted to know if he could live at home for as long as he wanted after he grew up. I said he could.

At the time, I found Peter's questions appealing, an affirmation that we had created a home he liked. I braced myself for his adolescence and a loss of those feelings, but Peter never turned on us. He just spent more time in his room and was less apt to come along on family outings.

Both Carolyn and Tom say that Peter was moody as a teenager, but we were not so much aware of this as of the fact that his conversation was reduced at times to his always humorous and often sharp-edged one-liners. His frustrations were released mainly on Tom, whom Carolyn now claims she thought he would kill at times. In actuality, there were no visible injuries and if their contests broke down, they were never suspended for long. Carolyn reported the scenes and we admonished Peter to be careful with his brother. There was a far greater size difference between them than four years would usually indicate, so I thought of Peter as a bear slapping out at an insistent mosquito, Tom. They would wrestle, Peter on his knees, a handicap which mainly served to give him more ballast. I was more concerned about the verbal cut downs, but Tom would not be protected. He entered the competition evening after evening, his face suffused with delight when he managed to come up with a remark we all deemed, "as good as one of Pete's."

At school Peter stuck with a small group of old friends and was wary of those who had already begun to drink and experiment with drugs. Carolyn, who had a picture of Peter at twelve on her bureau at boarding school, announced that her friends thought he was a "hunk." But Peter was not in the least ready to play the role that word implied. In fact, he would remain too self-conscious even to ask a girl for a date until he was almost eighteen.

He would have, at the time or perhaps at any time, been amazed to hear the view of a girl a year ahead of him. She wrote, after he died, a memory of Peter's seventh grade year.

> Donald, Cathy, Peter and I were all sitting around the pond waiting for a play rehearsal and discussing school ....Peter had the ability to describe the people and situations more accurately and more humorously than the rest of us.... Our comments were like filler. Peter saw the subtle, very telling things....His comments were those everyone wished they could have thought of.

Peter was going to boarding school for his high school years, as were most of his friends. Westminster had been familiar to us long before Peter applied for admission. Brooks had found himself there after his dismissal from a more prestigious school which he had loathed. In his day Westminster was known to be a good place to get a second chance and a good education. By 1981, the school had emerged from the difficult 60s and 70s with its traditions in tact and was more in demand ever than before. Peter was pleased to be accepted.

Westminster asked prospective students to describe themselves in writing using three adjectives. Peter was at first stymied by the request but after he and I talked the assignment over, he started to write, characteristically hedging most of his statements.

> The first adjective that came to my mind was talkative. Not in a rude way I don't think...This habit of talking can be an advantage or a disadvantage. Sometimes it can help me to know somebody better. But I can also say some things without thinking of the result.
>
> The next adjective I would use would be athletic. Not that I'm a superstar athlete; I do alright. I chose it to express my interest in sports. Ever since I was little I have loved sports....
>
> My final adjective would be concerned. I try to be aware and concerned about what is going on around me and how it could affect me...I also mean concerned in terms of how other people feel. If I see another kid being teased or pushed around, I try to imagine how that person feels...so therefore I, most of the time, don't join in.

Meanwhile in his final year at home, Peter spent much of his time with Tom watching TV and engaging in their usual impromptu contests. In the winter I heard the thumps of their wrestling matches and street hockey games in the basement and in the spring the sharp cracks of Peter hitting the whiffle ball from a flat space behind the house. It seemed that all his vitality and frustration went into those swings. I often looked out our bedroom window to see Tom, small and wiry, running into the tall grass to retrieve the ball, arguing all the while over his shoulder about the score and whether it was his turn to bat.

Brooks was still concerned that Peter had developed so few interests and lacked initiative. I was more inclined to believe that he was incubating and would proceed at his own pace. In any case, boarding school would lead him into increased activity.

It was just the kind of cool, sunny, autumn day on which a New England prep school is meant to open. As we crested the incredibly steep, curving drive which opens onto an enclave of grass and old trees, surrounded by sheltering buildings, a gawky senior greeted us. He led us through the well-ordered, 'new boy' steps to the infirmary with health forms, to the library for room assignments and class schedules, to the gym for towels and finally, to a reception on the headmaster's lawn. Peter was quietly polite, shaking hands and quickly stepping back.

We found his room and helped him unpack. Then as we walked away from the buildings and were halfway across the grass towards our car, Peter stopped. We both hugged him and he turned (he was already quite tall), lifted his shoulders and lowered his head in the way he always did when he wasn't sure of a situation, and walked back towards his dormitory.

I was worried and he was too, although we had not said too much about it, that he would be terribly homesick as he had been at camp three summers before. I waited three or four days. Then he called. "I'm okay. I'm not homesick. You're surprised, aren't you, Mom?"

The week before, as I was getting his clothes ready to pack, Peter had sat on the bed in our room and said, in response to some remark of mine about his going away, "You've brought me up for almost fifteen years and now you're afraid they might spoil all the work you've done."

Peter, who often seemed remote lying in his room reading magazines or watching TV with Tom, could surprise me with remarks like that. I had heard him do it to others, suddenly, perspicaciously, put himself in someone else's place. However, my worries were that Peter would not be happy or feel successful at school; I did not think anyone could spoil him.

A few weeks into the term, Peter's ninth grade advisor called us to report on how he was faring. Apparently, he was just beginning to loosen up, to smile. I think, based on the calls Peter made to us, that he had no idea that his wariness had been thus observed. But he did relax more as the routines became familiar, protected in a sense by those very routines and the fact that minor transgressions such as lateness and messiness, even smoking in the wrong place, were immediately erased by minor punishments in the form of work squads or restrictions to campus.

Peter was a watcher and in those first weeks, he did little else until some failing marks woke him to the fact that he must do some work in order to get his average into the safe middle ground. As his athletic ability still did not match his absorption with and encyclopedic knowledge of sports, Peter was put on the lowest soccer squad where his size at least gave him some advantage. He started very much as he would end at Westminster, in the background, while those who would become his friends began to discover and enjoy his wit. In his second year when we went to take him to lunch or dinner, he would often invite a friend or two to join us.

By the spring of his junior year, Peter was still running true to the comments made by his grade school teacher. When the details of second year algebra and a laboratory science course were threatening to scuttle his average, I wrote him a letter.

> Dear Peter—
>
> I'm sorry that you've had a bad half term and I don't doubt that you were working—results don't always immediately follow efforts...
>
> Although this is not a good time to have your record slip, it is not hopeless and there is point in trying to rescue as much as possible, not just for the sake of your grades but to prove that you can make yourself work in an adverse situation. When you were younger, you tended to be discouraged easily when something was hard to do—it is very important that you show yourself that you are beyond that stage. You can't expect miracles but with your other terms, you could end up with a reasonable average.
>
> Please don't let this defeat you. It would be such a waste of your very good mind.
>
> Love,
>
> Mom

When the police returned Peter's wallet to us, I found this letter folded into a small square in the corner of the billfold, some of the words faded out by water stains. The fact that Peter kept it for five years, moving it from wallet to wallet, seems more important than anything I had in mind when I wrote him. I was frustrated in his behalf that his intuitive, analytical thinking did not often win him recognition, and I wanted him to open doors for himself. Now it seems possible that in the message, my desires for him somewhat fortuitously met his need to see himself in a brighter light, a need held over from the chunky, little boy who seldom said, "Hey, look at me, Mom. See what I can do!"

The next September, I drove Peter back to Westminster for his senior year. He had been trying to see as much as possible of the U.S. Open Tennis on TV that afternoon, then we'd made unscheduled stops at two drugstores for basic items he'd forgotten like aspirin and toothpaste, so we were late. In the car, I issued some untypical warnings about drinking and pot. Peter's natural caution and relatively limited social life had meant that Brooks and I had not had to do battle with him on these classic issues of adolescence. In fact we had been glad when, at sixteen, he began to go out with friends more often even if it meant that he experimented more with alcohol and even pot. We had emphasized safety in terms of not driving when impaired and he had readily agreed. However, I was afraid that he could get caught "partying" at school and that that would be very damaging to him. He said he knew what I meant and the subject was dropped.

We drove up the hill onto what seemed an empty campus. Only the seniors were due back and Peter's classmates were already at a meeting. We hurried his things to a garret room in one of the oldest buildings where Peter and another boy would be in charge of younger students on their floor.

Peter was suddenly in the lofty position he had described to us when we had taken him out to lunch one Sunday early in his first year. Seniors, he'd said, could do everything from enforcing regulations on new students, with embarrassing if minor punishments, to commanding the biggest piece of cake at dinner. Because he had missed the opening meeting, Peter did not discover until twenty-four hours into his year-at-the-top that his leadership position was as head of a pit crew, who scraped plates and put them into the dishwashers—a steamy, greasy job. Peter wasn't used to giving orders to anyone except Tom, but after several occasions on which his crew was so slow that they were all late for their next appointments, he rose to the challenge. The day his gang beat everyone out of the kitchen, he reported the accomplishment to us with amusement and even, some pride.

Peter's calls reflected a new enthusiasm for the first few weeks of the year. He had been assigned to write up some varsity teams for the school paper; he might work on the year book; he didn't have to take any math or science. On the first day of classes, the teachers captured his imagination as they talked of broad concepts, and he was able to see how these overlapped from Economics to Ethics to Twentieth-Century History.

On a Thursday in early October a secretary appeared in my classroom at the day school to say that Peter was on the phone. She said he didn't sound well and thought I should speak to him right away. I hurried over to the main building and found that Peter was calling from the infirmary at Westminster. He had a severe sore throat and although the results of a test for mononucleosis had been negative the nurse felt he should be at home. I located Brooks at his antiques shop and he went immediately to get Peter.

At home Peter stood swaying in front of the TV in the basement because his throat was so swollen that that was the easiest position in which to breathe. We heard him in the night wandering in and out of his room. A second mono test on Friday also came out negative. Finally on Saturday when Peter felt he was going to suffocate, Brooks took him to the emergency room where a third test proved positive and he was given steroids.

For the next few days I cooked him mashed potatoes and he fell asleep whereever he sat down. But by the next weekend, one which the school had designated for seniors to visit colleges, Peter was well enough to make the trip to Washington D.C. which he and Brooks had planned. George Washington University had been my suggestion; I had heard about it from a friend. Peter needed another college on his list and he liked the idea of being in Washington.

They toured the buildings with a competent guide and a pleasant group of prospective students. Then, because it was a beautiful day, Brooks suggested they walk down the Mall and Peter was enchanted by the city. The university was one of the five schools to which he would eventually apply.

On his return to school ear infections plagued him for much of the fall and winter as they had the year before and the struggle to make up academic work took the bloom off his courses.

Peter knew that his grade average and extracurricular record were not strong enough to gain him admission to the kinds of colleges that, in his view, spelled success. So he had chosen five from the vast third category in Barron's bible of college rankings. His first two choices were colleges to which Westminster had sent a number of students whose academic records were similiar to Peter's and for which his test scores were more than adequate. But to be accepted at these, he would need strong recommendations from some of his teachers. Brooks, having written many such comments himself, felt that Peter's teachers would be hard put to know what to emphasize. We had listened, between the lines so to speak, in four years of parent conferences and sensed that the faculty were as mystified by Peter's abilities as by his disabilities, by his uncanny way of describing the forest after apparently missing most of the trees. His well-written essays on exams tended to come as a surprise.

Ethics was Peter's best subject in his senior year, so he asked that teacher to write for him. Although the recommendation was not strong in the current hyperbole of college admissions language, it shows a perspicacity about Peter and appreciation of him.

> Peter's greatest triumph was an essay he wrote on his exam...on self awareness....It exhibited a level of unity, clarity and thought different in kind not degree from those of the majority of the class.
>
> Peter never seemed to get into the mainstream at Westminster (a school with many social cliques) but rather maintains a few good friendships....I prefer to think of Peter's aloofness as representative of a character that is strong, sensitive and observant....

In April, Peter was wait-listed at one of the two colleges he thought he most wanted to attend and denied admission at the other. In the end, he was left to choose between a restrictive "general studies" program at Boston University and George Washington. His friend, Jeff, was going to BU but that was not sufficient to lure Peter, and he decided to set off for Washington.

I knew Peter was hurt by his rejections; he had even cried briefly over one of them, but I believed him when he said he wanted to get away from the fishbowl atmosphere at Westminster and I thought he would enjoy the freedom of a big city college. He had always been easily accepted by his peers so I presumed he would make friends in Washington.

Brooks, however, tried to influence Peter in two areas that spring. He wanted him to go to BU because he felt the familiarity of Boston and its proximity to home could make the adjustment to a big University easier. He also encouraged Peter to go out for varsity tennis in his final term at Westminster. Peter had played tennis for three years there and this was his only chance at a varsity letter, a recognition he had said he wanted. However, once Peter got back to school, he announced firmly that he was going to play baseball instead. As a senior he would automatically be placed on the Junior Varsity. We realized that he was avoiding the possibity of the humiliation of not making the top tennis team. Brooks said no more but took Peter out to lunch and bought him a baseball glove.

A few weeks into the term, Peter reported with delight a spectacular catch he had made in one of the team's practices, but the following week, he pulled a hamstring in his thigh so severely that it sidelined him and left him still limping as he went to receive his diploma in early June.

Brooks didn't get the movie camera focused in time on graduation day so it caught only Peter's back as he returned to his seat with a hitching walk. Then the film stuck. Brooks finally got it moving again for a few frames in which Peter, holding his diploma, towers over my parents looking more bemused than triumphant.

Four years later Tom walked the same stretch of lawn on his graduation day. My family were in the audience in larger numbers than might have been the case. All day they were carefully and correctly enthusiastic about everything. No one mentioned Peter.

I did not feel like screaming as I had feared I might. I watched Tom with pride, but as though from a great distance. He got the recognition he deserved in the end—a drama award and a *magna cum laude* diploma. I don't know how they arrived at the latter, after telling him he would not get a *magna*. Certainly, he deserved it for the record he held up to the time Peter died.

Brooks was really with Tom that day. He had liked Westminster as a student and kept in contact through the years, before the boys were there. Carolyn took a picture of them standing together, Tom very straight holding his prize and his diploma, Brooks leaning a little towards him.

When the ceremonies were over and Brooks and Tom were packing the car, I left them and crossed the grass rectangle at the center of the campus to stand for a moment in the place where Peter had said goodbye, hunched his shoulders and walked away on his first day at Westminster.

Brooks and I were keeping our memories to ourselves as we made our way back around familiar curves through pretty Connecticut towns, into the industrial center of Westfield,

Massachusetts, and out again to the cluttered strip where the boys had so often made us stop at McDonald's. Behind us, taking up the rest of the small station wagon, the final load of Tom's books, papers, recording equipment, pillows and clothes was indistinguishable from those of all the other years of such autumn and spring freights.

6

As the weather grew hot, I retreated more often to lie on my bed, in the mornings drawing the heavy shades against the eastern sun streaming in through two wide windows, and in the afternoons raising them halfway so I could watch the falling light on a green strip of mountain. Sometimes the dull hum of the lawnmower came through the window as Brooks circled the house in his battle to keep a carpet of grass amidst a hay field. In his fatigue that summer, he abandoned the farther reaches, even the boys' wiffle ball field, and by late July, our house from the road appeared to be marooned in a yellow-green prairie.

Brooks had always liked to mow but that summer he often found himself in tears on the mowing machine and knew he needed to get away to the small apartment he had rented in May. It was in Brookline near my parents' house and each week he went off with a carload of furnishings, unsold antiques, things we'd put away and even some things we hadn't. Months later, when I first saw the apartment, it was like stepping into rooms in a dream; boat pictures from the wall outside the guest room hung in the bedroom; a little table I hadn't noticed was missing stood beside a new, ugly sofa bed; the narrow bookcase from my childhood room was full of ornaments I hadn't seen in years, one of them a wooden bird on a piece of driftwood Carolyn had given her father one Christmas. Altogether, I thought, a montage of our shattering.

Once the beds he had ordered were delivered, Brooks sometimes spent two or three nights at a time in Boston. "Do you think you should be alone so much?" Carolyn asked. Being alone was becoming her greatest fear. Others voiced similar questions. Why wouldn't I like to go to Boston, see my family and an old friend or two?

My reactions were so far beyond most people's comprehension that I recorded them mainly to myself. Friends said things like, "Don't you want to get better?" I answered them in my journal. "They make it sound as though Peter's life and death were an illness I should recover from." I was not deliberately creating my thoughts and images of Peter; they were there in my mind and had to be allowed time and space. I knew that if they were in any way diverted or denied I would lose the only capacity I had to live with Peter's death.

I did wonder at first how I would pass the consecutive days alone, but I discovered a relief in being able to wander in and around the house talking to Peter, seeing him clearly in particular places. He tipped back in a plastic chair, his feet against the railing of the little porch off the living room, reading the sports pages in the sun. On the curving stair to the TV room he carried the cat carefully, his long fingers in her orange fur, suppporting her body in the fashion he had read was best for her.

"Pete, you are very much with me tonight. I have talked to you so endlessly since you have not been able to hear me. Everything I see and read and do ends up making me think of some aspect of your life, something that could have been different, something you will never get to do or see or know."

Around eleven at night either Brooks called me or I him. We recounted the small doings of our respective days, his mainly consisting of the difficulties of getting furnishings into an inadequate elevator.

The bedroom was often stuffy by then and I was not yet ready to try to sleep; so I went to the back room and sitting on the cool cement floor of what had been a garage, I began to work my way through Peter's belongings. The suitcases and crates which Wendy had packed and Brooks had retrieved from Peter's apartment back in March fit easily into an ell beyond a closet. Wendy had, at our request, given away his bed, nightstand and desk.

There was an immediacy in the items I sorted that no longer existed in Peter's room. There his bureau was almost empty, in the top drawer just a few camp badges, a baby picture, his Westminster diploma beside the box containing the elegant Gucci watch my mother had given him at lunch that graduation day, and in the lower ones odd pieces of shrunken faded clothing. The closet held one jacket and the remains of a complicated baseball boardgame. The bookcase held the books of his childhood reading. But here in the farthest corner of the back room were his college books, music tapes, bank statements, letters from friends and a whole stack of resumes newly minted for his summer job search. In December he and I had worked on a cover letter to a newspaper.

On the top of one suitcase a shirt I'd watched Peter open at Christmas was still full of pins and cardboard. Another suitcase was almost entirely filled with his athletic shoes, high tops and low, Nike and Adidas, Peter's only shopping indulgence. It had once been part of his job in a sporting goods store, to keep such shoes on display. "You can't sell air." Peter had said in an imitation of the manager.

Some of the clothes I could give away but the shoes would have to be thrown out.

On a dry, blue day near the end of August, I wandered down in the field to sit on a hay bale at the edge of the woods. There the midday sun touched my shoulders in a moment so reminiscent of old comforts that I could not stay for long. Fleeing the beauty of the day, I drove to town to the refuge of the soundproof booths at the Recording for the Blind studio where I worked most afternoons. There I was able to read aloud coherently while scenes of Peter's life, often triggered in unexpected ways by words in the text, passed behind my eyes. The reading done, I walked the streets on occasional errands, a new notebook for myself or a food item for Tom, who was home from his travels. One merchant observing my grim face and slowed step suggested to a friend of mine that I should be consigned to a hospital. When the friend, thinking that I was not fully aware of how I appeared, passed the message on to me, I pictured myself locked in a dark hallway at an institution, cut off from my house and from Peter's grave.

Peter's headstone had been put in place a few weeks before, and as soon as that happened, I was drawn to the graveyard every evening as the light began to fade. I went first to the terrace side of the house to pick a few blooms from among the fierce colors of Brooks' late summer garden. My path went by the school, through a development and across the lower road to the cemetery gates. By the time I climbed the slope to Peter's grave, my mind was usually back in January and engaged in a harsh dialogue.

"Why did you never ask him how he was really feeling in the two weeks after he told you of his anxiety attack? Why did you call Carolyn that Tuesday after Tom told Brooks that Peter had sounded bad?"

"How could you have known?" asked the few who, by some miracle of compassion, were still listening.

"How could I not have known?" I said to Peter as I stood by his grave in the dusk. In the fall I would end a poem:

> I tell myself the things I know
> She should have said to you.
> She was your mother.

Brooks, by then mistrustful of my sense of time, usually started pulling the evening meal together before I returned home. When I took over, he retreated to his chair in the living room with a drink and a cigarette. I could hear him talking to our black lab who slept at his feet.

When I called Tom from his room, he either took his plate upstairs and switched on a Red Sox game loud enough for us to hear it or he put on one of his CDs and sat down with us. He had rigged up a speaker in the hall and, for the three weeks that he was home, everything from Mozart to *Les Miserables* to Mexican guitar music throbbed through the house as if to banish echoes of Peter.

After dinner, Brooks and I watched a taped half hour of news in our room, talked to Carolyn on the phone and sometimes found another program to divert us. I looked forward to the sense of calm which usually came over me as eleven o'clock approached, another day completely over. Brooks wanted to sleep, or try to sleep, so I took my books and journals and went down the hall to Carolyn's room to take advantage of the night. As I lay on her low, wooden bed, a soft light brought the tiny flowers of her wallpaper close around me. My eyes raked the long shelves across from the bed which were filled with pictures, posters, little baskets, painted boxes, and odd congregations of animals of every size and material, from a floppy brown monkey to a minute glass bird in its nest.

When Carolyn was a very little girl, if anything was missing from around the house, we looked for it first in her room. She was (and is) a collector and almost everything she gathered followed her from house to house until she moved into her Boston apartment after she finished college. At that time, I had suggested that she sort and give away some of what she was leaving behind. But in the intervening three years, nothing much had been touched. Now, I was glad; I wanted to leave the clutter as it was, to borrow a few of the years reflected in my daughter's room.

I might as well. I could not give the room back to her (she said she could not sleep so close to Peter's door), anymore than I could give back the confidence that her brother's suicide had taken from her, or absorb for her the shocks she was receiving from a judgmental world. The first of these came from a young Irish friend who had written her several understanding letters about her loss, saying he wanted to hold her and comfort her. He had asked if he could come to Boston to visit her on his return to the U. S. in May. "It's the first thing I've looked forward to since Peter died," she told me. Then a mutual friend told Carolyn that the young man didn't know *how* Peter had died. She wrote to explain and did not hear from him again.

It seemed clear to Carolyn that this young man did not wish to be associated with her because of what Peter had done. Next a woman who worked with Liz told Carolyn she had been afraid to meet her because of what had happened in our family. By the time Carolyn started to look for a job, she had a strong sense that she would be discriminated against in many places if they were to find out about Peter's death and she carefully fudged the nine month gap in her resume. "It's like I'm a criminal because my brother killed himself." she said one night on the phone.

In the weeks before he left for college, Tom usually came in to Carolyn's room very late to talk. Sometimes he read me some of his poems. I tried to trace the thoughts behind his often seductive images, but my mind was too entrapped to grasp more than surface colors. It was the image of Tom himself that stayed with me; I had seen him bent over his desk writing by the light of candles set on a high shelf, their wax dripping down over the silver holders he had taken from the dining room.

One night, Tom picked up the enlarged photograph of Peter, at twenty, that I kept on a shelf near the bed. In it, Peter is sitting on our front steps, dressed to go out for dinner in a jacket that pulls tight across his big shoulders. He has his elbows on his knees, his fine, long fingers laced in front of him. His dark eyebrows lift a little to furrow his forehead above his glasses as he looks right at the camera with a gentle smile. Staring into his brother's face, Tom said, "He was so weak." He saw a look of denial cross my face and added quickly, "But you have to remember how I saw him, Mom, how big he was to me."

At such moments, I found myself asking Peter in behalf of both Tom and Carolyn, "How could you have hurt them so badly?" But as soon as I said it, I heard Peter's voice on the phone that January Sunday reminding me of the night we took him to the emergency room, asking in a typically oblique way for help.

Tom was due at college on a Tuesday late in August. On Monday afternoon, he packed the station wagon then took my car in town to do an errand on which he was gone much longer than we expected. Brooks was anxious to get going so as Tom returned, I started to ask, "Where were you?" but he cut me off. "I went to say good-bye to Pete."

Later, as I wandered around the house in its renewed silence, I thought that the journey to take our youngest child to college for his first year was one that Brooks and I should be making together. But such a trip that year would have cut too close to the memories of our trips with Peter four and then three years earlier.

The dormitory to which Peter was assigned at George Washington University is etched in both our minds, from the large young man standing in the lobby in his bathrobe with whiskey bottles bulging from his pockets, to the hot, rattling, overloaded elevators, to the dingy two-room suite on the top floor of the converted hotel. As Peter was the first to arrive in the suite, he put his things in the bedroom, but was quickly evicted by a girl who bounced in and announced firmly that she was reserving the room for herself and her boyfriend. Her boyfriend, it appeared, was one of the three returning students who had planned to room together. Peter and one other freshman had been added to the suite. Now six people would inhabit an area clearly designed for two or three.

Over lunch in a nearby restaurant Peter said, "It will be easier for me because I've been to boarding school." We did not contradict his vague statement but as Brooks and I drove north towards the Delaware motel where we would spend the night, we agreed that Peter's experience at Westminster wasn't going to stand him in good stead with the group to which he had been assigned. They were all city boys from New York and New Jersey. One of them had said to Peter, "Oh, ya, you're the guy from New England," in a tone that made it sound like a foreign land.

Peter called each afternoon that week from a pay phone in the basement of the building. "It's not at all what I expected college to be like," he told Brooks in a voice close to tears. We told him that we, too, thought he was in an uncomfortable living situation but encouraged him to wait and see.

The orientation period was disorganized and the University dining rooms were not yet open. A few times, Peter found people to have a drink or a meal with. He even signed up for a pub crawl in Georgetown and stayed the night at a different and 'nicer' dormitory. He inquired about switching rooms but was told his chances were slight. When he got his academic schedule, he was shocked to find that on the basis of one failed punctuation test, he had to take remedial English at eight o'clock every morning. He knew his English Achievement scores were high enough to keep him out of a remedial class, but apparently they were not with his records. I said I would arrange to have copies sent, but before I could accomplish this, just six days after he had arrived, Peter came home.

He called us at 7:00 A.M. on Saturday from the Union Station to ask for the train schedule from New York City to Hudson, NY. He then rapidly explained that there had been a small fire on his hallway the evening before. At dawn, he had woken up, decided not to stay, packed as much as he could carry and left the building unbeknownst to anyone.

Late that afternoon, Brooks drove to Hudson where Peter emerged onto the station platform bedecked with luggage, including his golf bag, which contained, among other unlikely things, blankets and his typewriter. On the drive home, he said, "I think maybe something good can come of this."

Brooks suggested that he might want to talk to a counselor, but Peter didn't feel he needed to.

At that point, I was relieved to see Peter. I had not been able to imagine him existing in the situation in which we had left him and although I would not have suggested such an abrupt flight, I had no inclination to make him go back. Brooks also accepted Peter's departure. He had called the housing office at George Washington the week before to object to Peter's room placement in terms of the crowding and the upperclassmen and been told that they could not help us, that room assignments were based entirely on smoking habits and music preference. Now his main concern was that Peter get started right away on something, anything, to prevent his slipping into a vacation lethargy of reading Sports Illustrated and watching TV.

Peter agreed and enrolled immediately in three courses at the local community college. In November, he took a job selling sporting goods. On the few weekends when Peter made plans to meet friends who were attending various colleges, I knew he was uneasy with them. I could hear him honing his story to make it sound reasonable. Then, over Christmas, Jeff told Peter that one of their classmates had dropped out of college, was working in Boston and looking for a roommate. Peter soon found himself a job in a big sports store in downtown Boston and moved in with Stuart. Jeff spent a good deal of time at the basement apartment, and the spring passed pleasantly.

However, Peter wasn't having much luck with college applications for the following year. In the fall, I had found a note pinned to his wall which said, "Don't fuck up this time." But as the rejections came in from several small colleges, I knew he felt he had done just that.

Peter sometimes went to my parents' house for Sunday lunch. One week his cousin Josh was there. Josh had just been accepted at Harvard so talk of colleges was as inevitable at that meal as the rare roast beef, potatoes, rice and peas. Peter ventured that he was still hoping to be accepted at Boston

College off their waiting list. My father's reaction was apparently immediate. "When I was at Harvard, none of us would speak to anyone from B.C."

Peter described the scene to me that evening and said, "I didn't mind because I don't respect Papa's opinion." But, for all that Peter didn't like my father's prejudices, he did want his good opinion. Perhaps that is why he signed up for courses at Harvard Summer School. We were surprised at his decision but pleased when, in one of the classes, he discovered how much he liked to write. My father, meanwhile, was certain that two good grades printed under Harvard's seal would serve Peter well someday, somewhere.

Less than a week after the classes ended, Brooks and I drove Peter five hours west into New York to Ithaca College, a place about which he knew little except that it was the only school that had accepted him. The college is set on a hill surrounded by a spectacular array of lakes and mountains. On a cool, misty Sunday, we carried Peter's bags to a double room in one of the stark towers which dominate the campus. We left him to embark on what appeared to be a well-planned orientation program.

The first call came at about 6:30 on Tuesday morning. Brooks talked to Peter and then called me to the phone. Peter had been awake for hours, walking around the campus smoking, waiting until he felt he could call. He was frantic. He said he could not stay at college. We tried to find out what was happening. There was no problem with his roommate and he was not disturbed about the academic courses he had signed up for. The problem was the dorm, he said. Most of the students were acting wild and out of control. He did not have specific examples. We persuaded him that he should make an appointment at the counseling office and told him to call again later in the day. He gave us the number of the pay phone just outside his room.

That day and the next we talked to Peter every few hours

from early morning to about 11:00 p.m. He was sleeping very little but he did go through the motions of buying books and attending the first classes. He saw a psychologist in the counseling office on Wednesday and reported that they had discussed whether or not Peter should stay at Ithaca.

"It isn't Ithaca; it's me, Mom. I don't know what's wrong with me," Peter said to me later that day. I was still trying to make him think about how he would feel about himself if he were to flee college after only a few days for the second time. I told him he would need treatment if he came home.

"You mean a hospital, Mom?"

"Well, not necessarily that."

On Thursday there was no call from Ithaca until mid-morning. A man's voice said, "Your son is in my office and he says that you have told him he can't come home, so he is going to jump from a building." It was the psychologist Peter had seen the day before. We talked for a minute and it was clear that he felt Peter was in no condition to remain at college. When Peter came on the phone I told him I would arrange to get him home the following day.

Brooks had taken Tom to Boston to shop for school clothes and go to a Red Sox game. When I reached him with this news we talked mainly of how to get Peter home. The bus trip was indirect and long and I did not want to drive leaving Carolyn alone at home. She was recovering from surgery to fuse a disc in her neck. We decided to have a car sent for Peter from the local limousine service.

In spite of her discomfort, Carolyn had written a long letter to Peter which he would never see. She was trying to repay him for a letter he had written to her from Westminster when she was miserable at college. She had been so pleased when he had cared enough to write and encourage her to stay at school.

Peter and I talked a few more times making arrrangements. "The doctor told me I need more coping skills," he said.

This man had said the same thing to me on the phone. I

had never heard those words used that way before. But I was to become very familiar with the phrase in the months to come.

Later, Peter would tell me that I didn't look at him when he first came into the kitchen after he had unloaded his things from the taxi. I was alone with Carolyn. Brooks and Tom were still in Boston. I remember that I reverted to an earlier role and told Peter he would have to pull his weight around the house.

He got up early the next morning. Desperate to keep moving, he offered to go to the post office to see if a package had come for Carolyn, then asked what else he could do. I said he could scrub his bathtub. I thought as I passed the bathroom door that his big frame crouched over the tub spoke his pain.

At midday, Brooks and Tom returned, and Peter insisted that Tom play one game after another with him until they finally drove off to see a tennis match. Late in the afternoon, Brooks, seeing the look in Peter's eyes, suggested a walk in the field. As they walked, Peter said he could not imagine what to do with himself.

Tom came into the kitchen while I was cooking dinner and said Peter wanted to take him to play miniature golf after we ate. He didn't want to go, because earlier Peter's driving had frightened him.

Peter left the dinner table early. As I was washing up, Brooks called to me to come up to the TV room. Peter was sitting in a big, red leather chair with his head down and his long arms dropped between his legs. He looked up at me and said, "My life is falling apart and I can't even cry." Brooks decided to call Peter's doctor. However, when he reached the answering service for our medical group, he found that his own doctor was on duty. He called us back and Brooks gave him a brief description of Peter's behavior. The doctor advised us to take Peter to the emergency room of the Berkshire Medical Center six miles away in Pittsfield, saying he would call ahead to tell them we were coming in.

It was one of those suddenly cold, clear nights of late

August, so I went to the closet and ripped Peter's ski jacket out of its cleaning bag. He put it on and went to our bedroom where Tom had fled to watch TV. Peter hugged his brother and said goodbye, adding, perhaps for the first time in their lives, "I love you." He went to the living room, gave Carolyn a hug and said the same words to her.

In the emergency room, Peter smoked and paced. He said the skin on his face was tingling. He could not stay still. After more than an hour, a nurse sat him down and, for a few minutes, seemed to hypnotize him. Another restless hour passed. We called Carolyn and Tom.

A nurse questioned Peter directly about suicide as we had not and he said he did not have a plan but could not deny that he had thoughts of it. She told us that if we took him home, one of us would have to be awake at all times. Since it was Saturday night of Labor Day weekend, he could not be admitted to the hospital for several days. The nurse offered an alternative, a crisis house run by the nearby Berkshire Mental Health Center. I don't know what we would have done if Peter had begged to return with us. That would have been the reaction of the Peter we had always known. But he did not ask. We heard the caution, the urgency in the nurse's tone and in our fear and fatigue we decided to let him go.

We waited again, and Peter paced until a pleasant young man came and led him away. When we got home, it was about 1 A.M. Carolyn and Tom were waiting for us in the living room.

Sunday and Monday were beautiful days. In the afternoons, Brooks and I went to a little, brown frame house on a back street in Pittsfield. Peter walked up and down the street with us, often holding his father's hand. Back in his room, he put his head in my lap and sobbed. I had not heard that deep, wrenching sound for about ten years. It was the sound that had often brought Brooks and me to Peter's room in the night to get him up, walk him around and talk to him until he seemed aware enough of his surroundings to go back to bed.

On Tuesday, Brooks accompanied Peter and a staff member from the crisis house to the Mental Health Center, where it was decided that he should remain at the crisis house until a hospital room was available. The next day, Peter said he felt a little better, and Brooks took him out to lunch. At the restaurant, Peter got up from their booth and went to speak to someone. When he returned, he told Brooks it was one of the people who had watched over him over the weekend. "I wanted to thank him for saving my life," Peter said.

Peter entered the hospital on Thursday, one week after I had received the call from the doctor at Ithaca and on Saturday I visited him in the afternoon. Although I had talked to him every day on the phone, I had not seen him since Monday because I had had to take Carolyn to Boston for her post operation check up and the hospital had not encouraged a visit on Friday.

The Berkshire Medical Center was very familiar to me as I had had three babies and an operation there but I had to ask the way to the psychiatirc unit. When the entrance door was unlocked for me Peter was waiting in a pleasant area around the nurses' desk. He said we could be alone in his room because his roommate was not there. Although he was fully dressed Peter lay on his bed as I took the only chair.

When I had seen Peter in the crisis house, I had not felt like crying perhaps because his distress there was so severe, but that day my tears came quickly to the surface. Here was the familiar Peter locked in the psychiatric wing of a hospital sharing a room with a strange old man. He was very much himself again able to tell me that the nurses and counselors were kind and to make observations about the sad stories of the people among whom he had been placed. But he knew that he would be there for about two weeks and he didn't ask to come home any sooner.

In the course of the next week, Brooks and I attended two conferences with and about Peter, each time seeing a different doctor and a different social worker. The first social worker told me that the staff did not think we needed family therapy and that Peter did not need medication. I questioned this second decision and was told that a blood test had determined that he did not need an antidepressant.

The psychiatric unit was peopled mainly by middle-aged and elderly women patients and activities there were limited. However, when a girl his age was admitted, Peter became interested in her. He even took comfort from the fact that an attractive girl had some of the same kinds of problems that he did.

When Peter had been in the hospital almost two weeks, I had an appointment with a Dr. Donald. He was the doctor in charge of Peter's case and also the head of the hospital's psychiatric unit. After an initial interview Peter had had little contact with him and neither Brooks nor I had met him.

By then, Tom was back at Westminster and Brooks and Carolyn had flown to London. We had decided not to change the plan for Brooks to take Carolyn first to London and then on to Galway where she was to spend the college year. She had been told by her surgeon that she could not travel until a week after the term began so there was no student with whom she could make the trip. Brooks was going to do some buying for his antiques shop and help her get settled. He would be away for a week.

For the first forty-five minutes of the appointment, Peter and I talked to one of the counselors. Then Dr. Donald arrived and breathlessly explained how busy he was because he was about to take a trip around the world. Peter had already described to me the weeping and wailing which the impending departure of this debonair doctor had engendered among many of his women patients.

When I realized that Dr. Donald expected me to take Peter home immediately, I objected as I had not been told that he was to be discharged that day, and was on my way to school. It was agreed that Peter could stay until the afternoon, but there was no time for me to discuss my concerns about his return home. He was to continue to see the therapist, Dr. Linder, to whom Dr. Donald had referred him without consulting us. As I left, Dr. Donald casually told me that Peter could always change therapists if he wanted to.

Although I had been told at the hospital that I should pursue my normal schedule, I did not go to any of the meetings that took place after classes. The demands of the school day took my mind off Peter but as I drove home the tension of living with him in his state of palpable misery returned and I played a necessary mental game. I tried to imagine where he would be when I arrived and in the process forced into my mind a vague picture of his body drowned in the swimming pool, knowing even as I created it, that I fully expected to be relieved of this tragic vision. Peter usually expressed his own relief at my return and, if I took a walk, he would go with me across the fields and into the woods.

In the evenings, we ate supper in Brooks' and my room, watching the news. Peter sat on the floor with the huge salads he made for himself. When we talked, he kept saying that he did not know what was wrong with him, what had happened to him. One night, I finally said something to which he replied, "Hold on to that, Mom. Keep saying it to me." I don't remember my words only that I reached him with the thought that what he was going through would someday end. But the sense of hope did not last and most of the time, I could not relieve his feeling that there was no way to get his life back.

At that point Peter was still restless and talked about getting a job although he did not equate this with the idea of "getting his life back." That, in Peter's lexicon, meant going to college and living as his friends were living.

Soon after Brooks returned Peter applied for and was offered a job as a busboy at an inn and at the same time was asked to return as a sales clerk to the sporting goods store where he had worked the year before. They had liked him and wanted to give him more responsibility. He fled the inn after two hours and the store after two days, panicked at the prospect of using new cash registers. Next, he volunteered at the town library, but when he began to run into people he knew, usually parents of his friends, he was embarrassed and stopped going after a few weeks.

Each time as Peter started out on one of these endeavors, Brooks and I expected that he would be able to handle it. The challenges seemed so slight, so well within his proven capacities. Certainly he was not doing as well as Dr. Donald had predicted at the hospital when he told me Peter's main problem was his inablilty to adjust to college. But the doctor was long gone and with each failure we learned a new lesson about what Peter could be expected to do in the near future.

Soon after Peter left the sports store, Brooks and I were scheduled to meet with Dr. Linder. During that session at which Peter was present, Dr. Linder spoke with a studied calm as he sought to neutralize each of our concerns. He stated firmly that he and Peter were making progress. But as we talked I was disturbed that after eight weeks he seemed to have so little sense of the importance of what had happened to Peter at Ithaca or even of the fact that going to college was something Peter had very much wanted to be able to do. After the meeting I began to inquire about other therapists, but I did not bring the subject up with Peter because I did not dare to undermine whatever support he was deriving from his appointments with Dr. Linder.

In the middle of November, when Peter's weekly routine had dwindled to two therapy sessions and several workouts at a health club, Dr. Linder suggested that he join a small therapy group made up of his patients. He told Peter that he had consulted the others, mostly women in their thirties, and they had agreed to Peter's joining them.

Peter was extremely agitated when he returned from the first meeting on a Friday evening. The next night, he slid to the floor against the refrigerator in our kitchen and told Brooks and me that he wanted to disappear.

1971

1970

1978

1979

1973

1981

1986

1988

7

AT THE BOTTOM OF A PLASTIC CRATE IN WHICH WENDY HAD packed the contents of Peter's desk, I found the cardboard backing and one sheet of a yellow legal pad. On this piece of paper Peter had written:

> Ithaca-Counselors talk with Mom/She knows better
> Waiting for the car not feeling anything
> Car ride-that morning. That morning.

There was no date on the page and thus no way for me to know when he wrote these lines. I thought at first that they could have been notes for a long piece which I know was written in the fall. But the words seem such an acute distillation of how Peter felt on leaving Ithaca that I now believe he wrote them right after he turned down the dorm room at B.U. and felt again a separation of himself from the person in the scene. He had said to me in describing his subsequent anxiety attack, "I felt as though I were watching myself." And written in his journal,"I mean, hell, it's not like I goddam threw everything away just because I decided I didn't want to move into the same room with a total stranger. But tell my body that."

I can be more certain, however, of when Peter worked on the description which includes his memory of "that morning' when he left Ithaca. Peter confided what he was writing about to a girl he had known the previous summer and she in turn wrote of this to Wendy a few weeks after he died.

The piece covers sixty pages of legal paper in his widely spaced, slightly rounded script. I imagine that he wrote this description during several weeks in October and early November before his time was taken up with end of term papers and exams.

In those weeks Peter was receiving frequent calls from Tom who, in his senior year at Westminster, was in a turmoil over college applications and his social life. Peter was familiar with Tom's propensity to dramatize, but something Tom said in a particular conversation must have set Peter to thinking about his brother in terms of himself and taken him back to the night two years before when he had told Brooks and me that he wanted to disappear.

> *"Count to seven, 1, 2, 3, 4....You're dead, you're lucky, so lucky...5 6, 7."*
>
> *Well, hell, that's certainly dramatic. Are you helping yourself when you say things like that? Why Tom? Why say something like that to yourself? Sure you have problems, big problems.*
>
> *"You're lucky, you're dead."*
>
> *Aw, cut the shit, Tom! It's too easy to say things like that. Respect your problems but don't put them on a pedestal. Don't make them bigger than you, than they already are. It's too easy. I know. I've done it myself.*
>
> *But you got to that point, didn't you, Tom? That station where the last vestige of enjoyment comes from saying things like, "You're dead, you're so lucky."*
>
> *Of course, it's easy for me to sit back and give you a hard time; probably too easy. So I'll do more than that, Tom. I'll go back to when I said the same sort of things.*
>
> *"You okay, Peter?"*
>
> *"What?"*

I heard her the first time, Mom.

"Peter, are you okay?"

"I don't know."

"Do you wanna talk?"

"I guess so..."

"How did it go with Dr. Linder today?"

"Nowhere."

"I'm sure you're bound to have sessions like that."

"Every one is like that."

"What do you mean, Peter?"

"Just what I said."

"You mean, you've seen him for eight weeks and gotten nothing out of it? I don't believe that. You just said last week that you had had a good talk with him."

"Yeah, well things change."

You gotta watch what you say, kid.

"What's changed, Peter?"

She's using your name. You feel ten years old. It's what you want, isn't it?

"What?"

Of course, I heard her.

"Peter, listen to me. What's changed?"

Mom's afraid of losing me. I can see it in her eyes. Making her feel this way is one of the few things I have left to give evidence of my existence. To make me feel, effect change, have some control.

"I don't know. I just don't care."

"Well, I do. What are you doing?"

"Trying to disappear!"

"Trying to disappear." Well, what do you think of that, Tom? I place my head between my hands and slide my back down the smooth surface of the fridge. I'm twenty years old and I'm sitting on the floor of the kitchen "trying to disappear." I've got problems too, big problems. But I'm still being dramatic, dramatic enough though. My parents are going out for the evening. Can a mother or a father go out for the night when their older son is scrunched up against the fridge "trying to disappear?"

"Peter, what is it? What's wrong?"

"I just..."

"Brooks...

"Yes."

"Come here."

"You were going to say something."

Yes, Peter, what were you going to say? Whatever it is, it better be good. Hell, you're already on the kitchen floor "trying to disappear" and Dad hasn't even seen you yet. You know this behavior is silly. You know you're going the wrong way. You know you're hurting yourself. Yet, you've become so scared and overwhelmed at the thought of turning around that you just keep going.

"I, I just wanna die..."

Have you ever said anything with less conviction? Do Mom and Dad sense this? Or are you safe, hiding behind something as scary as wanting to die?

"Peter, what are you saying...do you want to hurt yourself?"

"I don't know anymore."

"Peter, this is serious. Are you thinking about suicide?"

Well, there it is, Pete. They said it for you. They said it in a way that you don't even have to repeat it. You can just say yes or no.

"Yes."

That wasn't so bad.

"Peter, look at us. Do you hear what you're saying? I mean, how can you just come out and say this... Look at us. Do you have a plan...? How are you going to do it?"

Ooh, you're gonna have to be careful on this one, Pete. Answer the wrong way and they're gonna start talking about hospitals again or at the very least they're gonna call Dr. Linder. Then what? What do you say to him? 'Oh sorry to bother you, Dr. Linder. I'm just trying to make myself feel by scaring the shit out of my parents.'

I'm just like a little kid who is pretending to be sick to avoid going to school. Instead of pretending to have a stomach-ache or a headache, I'm pretending I want to kill myself. Instead of wanting to get out of going to school, I want to get out of learning how to live.

Come on now. You've gotta say something. This is getting complicated.

"I've just been thinking about it."

"For how long?"

"I don't know. I've thought about it off and on."

I'm not being evasive this time. I really don't know and it's an odd feeling. It's like waking up from a dream and being halfway convinced you've had the same dream before but you're not really sure.

"Do you want to talk to Dr. Linder? That might help."

Help. You guys don't get it, do you. I don't want help. Help means going forward. I can't do that. Can't you see that? I go to two colleges and spend a total of ten days. I come home and spend a total of two days at two jobs. And now, now I just walk around the house smoking cigarettes and watching T.V. Haven't you seen me? Help. Come on, can't you play my game? Can't you go about the house making it cozy, warm, and safe, only talking about nice simple things and let me slowly evaporate?

"Peter? Well, I think we oughta give him a call. Do we have his home number?"

Your mother is going to look for Dr. Linder's number. She's gonna call him unless you say something. Unless you say something, you'll have to talk to him. What the fuck are you gonna say to him? You have no idea, so say something now. Now!

"Dad, I don't think I need to talk to him."

"Peter, something's gotta happen."

"Why?"

"Peter, we had plans to go out tonight. We can't just do that when you're talking about suicide."

See, Pete, it can't be done. You just can't disappear or evaporate or whatever you want to call it. There is no such thing as leaving quietly. No matter how small you try to make your world, any decision you make, like not coping, will generate effects beyond yourself, especially when you're dealing with your parents.

How are they being affected? It's hard to tell. You see reactions but who knows what's fueling them. Mom's gonna call Dr. Linder. She and Dad are gonna try to cope for you, in spite of you, for your sake as well as theirs.

Does that make you feel any better? No. Does it make them feel any better? You don't even know. Why? Because you haven't really been thinking about what your behavior is doing to them? Been so busy trying to disappear down different chutes in your brain, you haven't had the time to think about anyone else. But now for some reason, it bothers you to hear that they might shun cocktails to sit home and make sure their older son doesn't disappear.

They're willing to make a tangible compromise for your sake. And that bothers you because you're not willing to do it for yourself.

Mom calls from the bedroom:

"Brooks, I've got Dr. Linder. Why don't you pick up in there."

"Okay."

Dad looks at me as he reaches for the phone. I know there is something wrong about this, and his eyes tell me that he does as well. He wants to say,

"Peter, you—not us—should be talking to Dr. Linder."

But he can't say it anymore than I could tell Mom it wasn't necessary to call Dr. Linder. Parts of both of us have become victims of our habits of behavior.

But so, so what? He's fifty-six and has had a fairly happy and productive adult life. You, on the other hand, are twenty, and you've not been able to make a step past high school. So fuck, if Dad can't bring himself to give you the phone. What counts now is whether you get up and take the phone.

But I don't. I just sit there staring at the floor, waiting to be talked about and feeling about eight years old.

"Well, obviously he's been down ever since coming back from school, but no, I wouldn't say I thought it was this bad."

Dad sneaks a sideways glance at me. He looks disturbed or disbelieving.

How has it gotten to this point? Am I really talking to my son's shrink while my son sits on the kitchen floor with his back to the fridge? Is my son really going to try to disappear? How did all this happen; when did it happen?

"Well, what we're concerned about at the moment is whether we should..."

I'm going to leave now. Leave the kitchen, that is. I don't want to speak to Dr. Linder. I also don't want to hear my father talk to him about me. So I'll just go out into the living room and imagine first that Mom, Dad, and the good doctor will come up with some wonderful plan for ole Pete. And then part of me will be immensely disgusted with how comforted another part of me feels at this thought.

I can't relax though in the living room because I keep picking up disturbing snippets of the phone conversation. Why don't you just go to your room and stuff your head between your pillows. Why? Because the more I hear, the more I want to hear, have to hear.

"Well, we've brought up hospitals..."

Hospital, hospital wouldn't do any good. Two weeks at Berkshire Medical Center didn't do shit for me.

Didn't do shit for you? For you? What did you expect it to do for you? Isn't that a big problem of yours, Peter? What's been done for you, especially by dear Mom and Dad, when things were a little too tough on you? It's too late for that type of realization now.

Okay, I'll go away for now. But it's not too late. It's just not time yet.

"What? What did you say? Really, I couldn't hear you." I mean, lately I've been pretending not to hear my parents. You know, to make them think I'm caught in some mystic mire, which they'd have to muck through if they were to reach me. "But really I didn't hear what you said."

Hey, don't worry about it. At least you're curious.

"It's just, you know, we're feeling a little hopeless at the moment, and..."

Don't say that, Dad. Maybe I heard you wrong. You didn't say that. Yes, you did. You know how scary it is for me to hear how scared you are? You can't be scared. If you are, what does that leave me with? Don't you remember when I called home from Ithaca? Don't you remember what I was doing? I was abdicating any sense of personal responsibility.

I said, "Mom, don't you see? I just can't do it here."

Note Mom, I said, "Don't you see?" I didn't just flat out say I couldn't make it. I asked you 'to see' that I couldn't make it. I wanted you to validate my leaving Ithaca. Take responsibility for it. But you were smart that time. It seemed to me as if something suddenly clicked in your head. You said to yourself, "No, this is wrong. It isn't Ithaca and it wasn't George Washington either. It's Peter. I can't tell him it's all right to come home."

On the other hand, maybe it wasn't something that had just "clicked" with you, Mom. Maybe you had known it for a long time or at least strongly sensed it. "Something is wrong with Peter. He's alive but for some reason, he's not living. If he comes home from Ithaca, he'll be even more lifeless. There is no way I can condone this."

You saw how damaging it would be for me to leave college a second time? Whether or not it was a mistake not to have made me stick out more things when I was younger, wasn't important now. The point was you had to make a stand. You did. But it didn't help, at least not then. Because I had already made up my mind that I was helpless to deal with college.

"Peter, you're an adult now. It's not for me to say come home from college or stay at college. That's up to you."

So I came home, supposedly because it was my decision to do so.

There was that wonderful paradox. By merit of my age and supposed capabilities, I was the one to make my own decisions. Yet at the same time, I didn't have the coping skills to deal with one week of college.I felt in my stomach more than nervousness, almost as if two extremes were tearing me apart.

I had two feelings going against each other. But the first one, that I should stay at Ithaca, was a tough feeling to act on. It required initiative, patience, perspective, toughness to make it grow in strength. These ingredients were not naturally at my disposal, and I didn't yet know where and how to forage for them. On the other hand, the feeling that I couldn't deal with Ithaca grew quickly and effortlessly until it was painfully lush and strong and I was hopelessly tangled in its roots.

Maybe that's why I consciously decided to abdicate responsibility for myself. Maybe I realized somewhere inside that I would need help to break the grip of these roots. On the surface though I didn't see it that way or feel that way about it. And when I did it, made that decision, I felt strange, a way I never felt before.

I'm walking around Ithaca College waiting to go home. A couple of hours ago, I told a college counselor that I might try to kill myself if I had to stay here. I also told him my mother didn't want me to come home. He called Mom and told her it wouldn't be a tragedy if I left Ithaca. It might be best since I was talking about suicide. Mom knows coming home will just make things worse, but this is the first time I've put suicide on the table. She's not prepared to call me on this. I'm not surprised. Well, it's done now. Save me signing the withdrawal sheet.

This is when the feeling first hits me. I feel this eerie separation from what I'm doing. I see my hand signing my name but it doesn't feel like I'm the one in control of it.

After I sign it though, the feeling subsides. For a short time as I leave the counseling office, I feel maniacally happy. But this happiness has no roots. There's no room for them even if they existed.

As the happiness moves out, melancholy follows on its heels. I'm walking around the campus and realizing that none of it matters to me anymore, that I didn't overcome anything here. I just wrote it out of my life. As I look at the people walking around me, I feel not so much that I don't fit in, but that I don't even exist to them that I can see them but they can not see me. I wander around wondering whether my feet are even stirring pebbles.

So you see, Dad, while it's easy, too easy in many ways, to back out of responsibility for your best interests, it is by no means a painless process. Now I'm looking to you, Dad, you and Mom as the two people who will prevent anything really horrible from happening to me. Of course, at the moment, we have very different ideas of what's horrible. But I'll get back to that later. What matters now is that you're scared, aren't you Dad? You, Dad, for me an embodiment of an ideal, however unhealthy, is scared. And what's the ideal?

Well, it grows out of and glows from that house. The house I'm in now, the house the family has lived in since I was six. From the start, it was one of the nicest houses on the street. The importance of this being that it made the house different. It helped to isolate it from the other houses. The house was also set back from the street and surrounded by eight acres of land. This by itself was enough to separate our home from the rest of the street. As it was, the street itself didn't offer a bustling neighborhood network. But no matter. Our house wasn't going to be involved either way. Our house was about the business of offering a self-contained existence. Dad's an antique buff so the house was always beautifully decked out. Yet, at the same time, it beckoned with comfort. What resulted was a place that happily made allowances for living in the past or in an unfounded future, but very rarely in the moment.

The big problems, the ones that were gonna effect me for a lifetime didn't seem too capable of drawing attention to themselves in this house. Sure Mom and Dad would bring them up and try to impress certain things upon me, but they might as well have been fir-

ing blanks. I didn't care about getting involved with an outside activity or planning my summer, or…I had that house to go to with its warmth and a friendly dog who let me lie on his stomach, cable tv, a little brother who wanted to be interested in everything I was. And who knows, maybe the house wouldn't have seemed so strong if my parents had pushed harder. But wasn't it inevitable that they wouldn't. I mean, after all, wasn't the house their creation, a manifestation of their personalities? It was initially, but for me, it became bigger than them.

The house made me think it was easy for all of us not to push out and away from what we knew. But Dad, and you too, Mom, know now that, in my case, things have gone too far. So you're scared Dad, not only because you realize this but also because you hope things haven't gone too far for you. You're wondering whether the attitude radiated from the house has such a sure hold on you that you won't be able to push me, push yourself.

The way I see things now, if you hadn't been scared then I might have been just left alone to shoot the rapids and eventually do something really stupid. But there is limited value in imagining how things could've been, worse then they already were.

"As I said, Dr. Linder, as far as tonight on a practical level, we don't know whether we should leave Peter alone."

God, you see what comes of sitting on the kitchen floor and talking about suicide? Your parents end up asking a diminutive Jewish man in his early thirties whether it would be all right to go out for drinks while their twenty-year-old son stays at home.

You're trying to fit in somewhere that you're far too big for now, Peter. You're working on being six years old, but you can't escape those fourteen years change.

Now who knows what Dr. Linder has been saying to Mom and Dad? But whatever it is, Dad is now motioning to me to come in the kitchen. Right away I'm almost positive that he wants me to take the phone and do some talking of my own. I think for a moment about simply running to my room but I don't because I'm stuck with one of those slivers of reason that make it impossible for me to be six years old again.

If you run to your room, one or both of your parents will come to get you. This will involve asking Dr. Linder to hold on because Peter, the young man who manages to drag himself into his office two days a week all by himself, had opted, instead of talking to him, to run into his bedroom.

That scenario in and of itself is enough to discourage my mad dash.

"Peter, he wants to speak with you."

What will you say to that as you lie on your bed? You know you will feel desperate because you will have already sunk to the level of running to your room. But it's been all for nought. So now what? Do you try to run through your bedroom wall? No, you start pulling that shit and you'll find yourself in the big leagues, fast. "One Flew Over The Cuckoo's Nest," straight jacket, the whole bit.

So there is Dad, motioning me out of the living room. Maybe he doesn't want me to talk to Dr. Linder. Yes, he does. Anyway, it's gotta be better than running through walls. I start to walk into the kitchen over to where Dad is on the phone. I feel sluggish and aimless. My legs are weak. Maybe I am beginning to disappear.

Dad extends the receiver toward me. His eyes look very sad.

"Dr. Linder wants to talk to you for a little bit."

Silence.

"I think you should, Peter, just for a little bit."

He said, "just for a little bit" twice. That makes me feel more comfortable about talking to Dr. Linder. He would say the same thing to me when I was younger. Piano lesson's a bitch. "Just do it for a little bit, Peter." "A little bit" meant I really didn't have to try too hard and whatever happened really didn't matter because Dad would say it was all right to stop and come home.

I don't know if Dad really thought it was all right to stop and come home but that's the way he made me feel and that was all right with me.

You're going to talk to Dr. Linder, but not in the kitchen. You've got two separate acts to maintain one for Mom and Dad and one for Dr. Linder. You could blow your act with Mom and Dad if they hear you talking with Dr. Linder.

"Okay, I guess so. I think I'll go upstairs though."

"Okay."

Going upstairs also gives me some time to decide how I'm gonna act and what I'm gonna say to Dr. Linder. He's been getting second-hand samples of my fridge schtick from Mom and Dad. What's he gonna think of that shit? He knows me as a confused young man who comes to see him twice a week. I come into his office and I sit tense and uncomfortable because the love seat is too forgiving to my weak back. He looks at me from the moment I sit down while my eyes sweep from him to my hands to his office decor and back again. If this goes on long enough, he will shift his weight in his seat, hunch his shoulders forward, curl his lips in a puzzled grin and ask me,

"Well, how are things with you?"

"Not too bad, I guess."

God, somehow I could spit that same hollow answer out week after week, without choking on it. It meant absolutely nothing to me when I said it. Who knows what Linder made of it. Who knows if it would have made any difference because at that time I was in my "I wanna be wherever I'm not" stage. At therapy, I wanted to be home. At home, I wanted to be in town. In town, I wanted to be at home, with each move hoping I could find someplace that required nothing of me; a place I could enjoy and feel comfortable in without having to offer a thing.

So I would go through therapy with my mind somewhere else.

"Your mother was making you crazy, wasn't she…"

"I don't know. Maybe. Yeah, I…"

Who cares if she was or she wasn't. It doesn't matter. You're not on the right track anyway, Linder. What is the right track? I don't know. In fact, at this point, I strongly suspect that one doesn't even exist.

"So, how do you think starting up classes again will be?"

"I don't know. I really…"

You think I'm gonna take classes at the goddamn community college? What are you talking about? If I'm gonna have to do work somewhere, be uncomfortable and isolate myself from people somewhere, if I'm gonna have to walk around chain smoking and talking to no one and feeling like a martian, I sure as hell ain't gonna do it at the fucking Community College!

Of course, I didn't say something like that to you, Linder or to Mom and Dad because I knew no answer to the response that would inevitably ensue.

"Listen, taking classes or not taking classes is totally up to you. But if you're gonna live in this house, you gotta do something."

So I play ball instead with Linder, with Mom and Dad, and

with myself. Except, as I said, I've got different ball games going with Mom and Dad from the ones with Linder. I can float through his office twice a week for close to two hours without showing him that I want to disappear, but not with Mom and Dad. I see them every day and night. And from time to time, the desperation wells so strongly in me as I stare blankly into the T.V. screen, that I have to touch them in some way, even if it ends up hurting them, scaring them. This time, it was too much for them though, and they had to take their hurt and fear to someone, to Linder. And now I have to explain it to him. It's embarrassing enough trying to disappear in front of your parents, but now I have to explain it to some therapist I've done little more than go through the motions with for six weeks.

Sitting down in Dad's old red chair. It's half vinyl, half leather. Placing my right hand on top of the receiver while I curl my fingers over the mouthpiece gently, lifting it off the cradle.

"I got it, Dad."

***

"Mike, how are you?"

"Oh, I'm getting along. And yourself?"

"Ah, I really can't complain. Well, actually I could, but I'm sure after a long week that's the last thing you want to hear."

"You do have something there."

"Has it been an especially trying week?"

"Well, my boundaries, the clear cut ones that I keep between my job and my personal life, that I brag about, well, they're getting fuzzed up lately."

"Hey, well..."

"Aw listen, that's not what I called to talk about. Now how about giving me another shot at you on the courts?"

"Fine by me, if you think you're ready."

"I'm ready. You worry about yourself. Tomorrow at four. Sound good?"

"Should be no problem. I'll see you there, Mike."

"Great, see you then Peter."

***

Well that sounds about right. Don't you think so?

I mean Christ, I'm sitting there in that chair and I'm hearing myself say, "I got it, Dad." Just like I've sat and said so many times before. And I just can't help expecting that the conversation is going to be like all those times before. Where do you wanna play? What time does the movie start? Is Chris around? Do you have any weed?

And though I've imagined it could be, it's not like that this time. I'm not talking to Ted or Jeff. It's Dr. Linder. He's a psychologist, Peter. You see him twice a week. His name is Mike, but you don't call him that. And he certainly doesn't call you about playing tennis. In fact, he didn't call you period. Your parents called him because they're worried about you disappearing.

Okay. Somewhere inside of you you know that much. Now talk to…

"Hello ah, Dr. Linder?"

"Yes, Peter."

Silence.

"Your father and mother are pretty upset, scared."

"I know."

"Well, what's this about suicide? It hasn't been coming up in our sessions."

"I don't know. I, I've just thought about it."

"Does this have anything to do with the group, what went on there?"

"I don't know…"

"Well, you were crying. Something was going on."

That's right. I was crying, wasn't I. Sitting in a circle with four total strangers and Dr. Linder.

"Well, as I'm sure you've noticed Peter is here for his first time."

"Hi, Peter. I'm Ellen."

"Hi."

"Hi, my name is Nancy."

"Hi."

"Nice to meet you Peter. I'm Ruth."

"Hi."

"Good to meet you. My name is Peter too."

"Oh yeah, hi."

"Have you been seeing Mike for long?"

Mike, uh oh, so she is on a first name basis with Linder. That bothers me for some reason.

"Ah, about eight weeks."

"He got you into the group pretty fast...You didn't even mention the group to me for two-and-a-half months and then it took you another three to get me here. So what does that mean Mike? Who's in worse shape, Peter or me?"

"I don't really think it's a question of that."

"I know. I'm just kidding around like I always do. Isn't that right, Nancy? Either that or I'm sleeping, right Nancy?"

"Peter, I told you I didn't mean what I said about that."

Silence...

(Shit. That's right. This thing goes for an hour and a half.)

"So why'd you want to see Mike?"

"Ah..."

"If you don't feel like talking about it yet, you know, don't..."

"Oh sure, Peter. I don't mean to push..."

You didn't want to come to this fucking group in the first place. Well, honest! You're not sure about that, which makes sense considering you've gotten to the point where you can't even make up your mind about what sneakers to buy. But now that you're here, you want to be somewhere else? You're not though, and you'd certainly feel embarrassed to get up and leave. So, if you're gonna be sitting here with these people for the next, Christ, seventy-five minutes, you might as well reveal something about yourself. Go ahead. Give them a piece of yourself. It's group therapy, not a job interview.

"No, that's okay. I mean, I'll probably feel a little more comfortable once I've said something about my situation. I guess things started when I first tried to go off to college. It was at George Washington University in Washington. See, I came from a small private high school in Connecticut and I guess you know that didn't help when I got to George Washington. I didn't realize how overwhelming it would be and I...I...I..."

"Believe me, Peter, I know how tough college can be for freshmen, going from home and all the new faces and red tape. It takes people a while to get adjusted."

"Yeah well, that's ju...just...just it. I, I didn't even give my, myself a chance t...to..."

Well, there it is now. I'm crying. The more I try to say, the more I cry. Remember though, crying is good. It means you're not holding back. Well, I don't feel there is anything productive about this particular cry. It's reflecting what a complete directionless mess I've been ever since I went away to school six years ago. And the worst part about it is I didn't even realize it then. And now that I have, I'm convinced there is nothing I can do about it, which in turn makes me feel incredibly depressed and devoid of any vitality. Yeah. Crying is definitely therapeutic.

"It was just hard sitting there for the first time and having to tell everybody everything."

"Well, that's not surprising, and we can talk about it on Monday."

"Yeah, I guess…"

"So, you think you can make it to Monday then?"

"Yeah, I can make it until then."

That wasn't too hard to say yes to. In fact, it was nice to say yes to. He was just asking me if I could make it to Monday. Hell, I've been wasting away weekends in front of the T.V.. set for years. It's never been a problem. And now, now somebody is asking me to do it as if it's some sort of task, as if I should feel some sort of sense of accomplishment in doing it. Of course, maybe that was Dr. Linder's intention when he selected his words.

He knows as well as I do that I haven't really stuck anything out or gotten anything done in about three months. So this is how to stop Peter from scaring the shit out of his parents and give him a sense of functionalism.

Just make it to Monday. Two days. The weekend. Smoke a lot. Watch football. Avoid extended eye contact with Mom and Dad, and before you know it, Monday. And what happens Monday? Well, you can't think of that specifically because then you'll realize that it will be nothing that couldn't have happened the last Monday and then you'll have no choice but to start thinking and probably talking about suicide again. That card has already been played for this weekend though. So instead, don't try to think about what will happen on Monday. Just maintain some misty fantasy in the back of your head. The kind of fantasy that takes in half-formed groundless notions and uses them to keep you going for a while, at least, until Monday.

"Now, how about your parents. What about calming them down?"

"Yeah."

"Just let them know things are going to be all right this weekend."

"Okay."

"I'll see you on Monday then."

"Yup."

Oh, Mom and Dad by the way, Dr. Linder and I talked it over. You should go out tonight because I'm not going to kill myself this weekend.

"He's still on the line, isn't he?"

"No, we're done."

"Peter, we still wanted to talk to him."

"Well, I'm sorry. I wasn't thinking about that."

"Well, uh huh, what did he say?"

Gosh, poor Dad. Listen to him. He really doesn't know which way is up anymore. Here he is, fifty-six years old and three-quarters retired. He's got just about every piece to the puzzle he wants. I mean, sure at one time, he probably envisioned a bigger, more exciting puzzle but hell, that makes him a lot like a lot of other people and it certainly doesn't give him any cause for shame. And besides, he's been able to bolster himself further over the last couple of years by imagining new possibilities and motivations arising around and within him once he and Mom have the school year to themselves.

It should have happened last year. Thank God for prep schools. Uh, but that didn't turn out to be the final liberator. Nope, uh, uh, because Peter went and ended up at the wrong college. Just not his type of place. Not his type of people.

Well, anyway, Peter comes back home and the empty nest is put on hold. Now I don't know how Dad felt when I came home that first time. Whatever the feelings, I'm sure they were mixed. Maybe he was feeling that way one does when one has been both apprehensive and anxious to face a challenge. But then, for one reason or another, the challenge is postponed or cancelled altogether. And in reaction, one feels both a sense of relief and a let down.

Regardless, I know this time, this second year when all the elements for the empty nest seemed to be in place that Dad was ready for it, welcomed it, wanted it. The puzzle for whatever it was worth was ready to come together. Yet before it ever got a chance to do so, this big old piece showed that it not only wasn't part of the puzzle but was also able to keep the proper pieces from coming together.

So here are Dad and Mom, but Dad most of all because he is capable of being optimistic. So it was harder for him when I came back home. Nothing left to do but absent-mindedly scratch the base of his neck and stare at the hard wood floor which needs to be polished soon.

He's got to be feeling like this problem would be shitty enough as it is if the parent and child relationships were still clearly defined. If I was sixteen or so and Dad and Mom and some doctor could just touch heads and say it was best for me at the moment if I went someplace for a while, you know, a hospital or something.

But I'm twenty not sixteen, and I should be calling my own shots, right? That's the way Dad always thought it would be. And why not? His own experience at being twenty and everything he's ever seen, heard, or read about twenty-year-olds says they're grownups. Grownups don't sit in their parents house day after day doing nothing.

So Dad's going, 'God is this my job?' It's like it's Christmas morning and he finds himself sitting in front of some colossal recreational contraption bought by grandma for Tommy, "assembly required" stamped in insensitive black letters on the box. Whatever it is when it's done, it will be too big to fit anywhere. So Dad, where to start, why start? So your older son won't disappear, or just to help his habit of letting other people put his pieces together for him?

"He wanted to know if I thought I'd be all right until Monday when I have my appointment with him."

"What did he mean by all right, honey?"

"I guess, you know, if I can just manage to keep things together."

Things? What things? Your life is fairly devoid of things. For you not sitting on the T.V. remote control when you flop down on the T.V. chair constitutes keeping things together.

"So, Peter, where does this leave us? Twenty minutes ago you were talking about suicide."

"I know that."

"Peter, you have to think for a minute how it sounds to us when you talk about wanting to be dead. It's very scary. I mean, we don't know what to believe, what to do."

"Go out for drinks. Don't worry."

"Now cut the shit, Peter. When you say it that way, it sounds like you're trying to get rid of us so you can, can do something."

"I'm sorry. I mean you can go out. I'll be all right. I'll just watch some T.V."

That sounds nice and cozy, doesn't it? Just stay home from life and watch a little T.V.., kill a little time until Monday when... when...aw, just kill a little time. That's good enough.

"Are you being honest, Peter? Now really honest?"

Now the more I think about it, maybe Dad is partially right. That is, now I do want to get rid of my parents for a while. Not so I can hurt myself though, at least not physically anyway. It's not so much anyway that I want to kill myself. It's more that I can't live with the way things appear to me. The problem is I don't know how to escape life as I see it. Killing myself, no matter how much I'd like to convince myself it is, is not an option for me. I simply don't have it in my make up to kill myself. At this point, this particular Friday night. I don't know that, but in me somewhere I sense it.

But no matter. Even if I had it in me, I still couldn't do it. Suicide, like most other decisive actions, requires initiative for it to become realized.

Now considering that for over the last month and a half I've barely been able to muster enough conviction to wipe my butt, the chances are I won't be able to get my act together to kill myself.

However, I'm not yet thinking of suicide in such realistic terms. More than anything else, it's just a symbolic escape hatch; my foolproof last out of everything.

For now though, my standby temporary out, T.V. will do just fine. At least until Monday. T.V. is best as an out though when it's just you and it. It's harder (to leave) when your Mom pops in and out of the T.V. room to see if you've disappeared yet.

"Yes, I'm being honest, Mom."

I don't look her in the eye, though, and I'm not quite sure why.

My parents will go now, and not so much because I said it would be okay but more because somewhere inside they also know I couldn't kill myself.

"Okay, Peter. We'll be back around 8:30. If you want to call us, the number is right next to the calendar."

When my older sister and I were left to watch the house and our little brother, Mom and Dad showed us the number to call if we needed to reach them.

"All right."

"Okay. If you could just remember to turn the potatoes off at 8:00. Be back before you know it."

"Yup."

8

WE STAYED ONLY ABOUT AN HOUR AT THE COCKTAIL PARTY ON THE night when we left Peter to watch TV and turn off the potatoes. Brooks and I each had a sense that the immediate crisis had passed but the next day, a Sunday, we were nervous about his driving alone and much to his annoyance, followed him to town when he went to buy cigarettes.

Tuesday, when I returned from school, Peter was pacing the living room in fear that Jeff would call because it was the start of the Thanksgiving break. But Jeff had been told about Peter's condition. Tom came home that day and Peter became calmer as they fell into some of their old routines. However, when I drove Tom back to school, he said he had felt all weekend as though he were the older brother.

One night soon after the holiday Peter showed his father a scratch on his wrist which Brooks thought the cat had made until Peter explained that he had made it with a razor blade. I removed the package of blades I found in his room, although this was a foolish precaution as he had access to stores. However, the act of cutting himself was one I felt quite certain Peter would never carry out.

Peter and I had more conversations about his sessions

with Dr. Linder which were similiar to the one he would write about. When I suggested that he might like to see another doctor, he said no. It was clear that the idea of starting therapy over again seemed insurmountable to him. Brooks and I, however, were so frustrated by the lack of urgency in Dr. Linder's approach that we began to seek the advice of other professionals.

We questioned Peter's regular doctor to find out if his recent history of long term infections could have any bearing on his present condition. The doctor could see no connection.

A friend had recommended a psychologist with whom we had a couple of consultations. We both thought she quickly gained a good understanding of the essentials of Peter's situation and of ours and were glad when she offered to talk to Dr. Linder for us. This, of course, was pointless as he only assured her that Peter was making progress and cautioned that their therapy would take time. When we asked what was meant by that she said that two years would be normal in cases like Peter's. She hoped we would not rush towards hospitalization as she felt that experience in itself could do him harm.

A few weeks later an acquaintance, a man with long experience as a psychiatrist in a mental hospital, said just the opposite. He felt that Peter was bound to have another crisis and that we should not try to act as his "nurses" as he put it. Peter, supported by Dr. Linder, was begging us not to send him to a hospital again. When we talked to Dr. Linder on the phone he again counseled patience but agreed that Peter should make some plans for further activities in January, either a job or some courses at the community college.

By the second week in December Peter seemed a little better. He had resumed his limited daily routines and each evening he ate with us, helped me clear up, then retreated to the TV room. Later, if he wandered down again, either he or Brooks might suggest a card game. They sat at the kitchen table quietly laying out their Rummy hands, Brooks jotting down the running score to which neither of them paid much attention.

We were considering cancelling the reservations we had made for ourselves and the boys to visit Carolyn in Ireland over Christmas. Then Peter strode into the living room one day and said to both of us, "I can go on the trip. I won't spoil it."

In the ten days we were away in Dublin and then London, Peter held himself together. He joined us on all occasions even accompanying Carolyn and her friend Liz to a pub. I asked the girls how he seemed to them and they said they felt he was making a big effort to take an interest in their lives. I was encouraged that he was able to do this. Only Tom, who shared a room with his brother and who was the person with whom Peter was least able to pretend, heard a deadness in his voice and a sense of defeat in his words.

Three weeks after we returned, Peter doggedly went back to the community college he had attended for one term the year before. One night after the first few days of classes, he stopped at our bedroom door to tell us about an assignment he was preparing in his English course.

When I pass by the living room in the early mornings and see Brooks sitting at the far end of the sofa with his breakfast coffee and a cigarette, I know that sometimes he is seeing Peter as he was on the morning of January 22, 1987. He came striding through the double doorway, his shoulders hunched, saying that he had seen two men in his room who had told him not to go back to the community college. It was a Thursday, the day after he had told us about his English course.

Brooks called to me sharply, and as I came out from the bedroom, Peter was pacing, saying over and over that suicide was the only thing for him to do, that it would solve everything. I tried to stop him in one of his swings around the room. He loomed in front of me briefly; I looked up into his eyes and realized with a sense of hollow fear that he was not really seeing me.

I had been scared for him before, but at no time had I been totally unable to reach him. We called Dr. Linder. He agreed to see us right away. We drove to his office with Peter in the back of my two-door car, leaning towards us from the middle of the seat, continuing his litany of suicide.

In an old office building on the main street of Pittsfield, we followed Peter up stairs and down hallways, then waited while he went in to talk to Dr. Linder. When we were ushered in, Dr. Linder immediately said that he and Peter had agreed that Peter had not seen two men in his room. Peter was quiet, deep inside his misery. Dr. Linder hurried to a phone at the back of the room.

We could hear that he was unable to get a room for Peter at the Brattleboro Retreat in Vermont. He then called the Mental Health Center, which had taken Peter into their crisis house in August, and told someone there that we were coming over.

I left Brooks and Peter in the waiting room at the Center to drive home and then to school with assignments for my classes. As I drove back to the city, huge flakes of snow raced towards the windshield. My mind was on getting back to Brooks and Peter. They were standing in the parking lot as I pulled in. On the way home Brooks told me that the psychologist they had seen had told him Peter had to be in a hospital and that he would call us as soon as he found a placement for him. Peter was completely quiet. It was snowing so hard that we decided to stop in town for the paper and something for dinner. I stayed in the car with Peter because, although I did not feel that he had any intention of trying to get away from us, I didn't want him to be alone.

More than a foot of snow had accumulated by mid-afternoon, when a man called from the Center to say that McLean Hospital near Boston had a room available for the next day. He urged me to get Peter there as soon as possible and said he thought Peter should spend the night at the crisis house. But the roads were impassable, and Peter was calm and reachable again. He did not raise any objections to going to the hospital. In the evening he ate dinner with us as usual and then packed a suitcase. Outside a plow cast an eerie light on the huge banks of snow it was piling behind the house. We took precuations as we had been advised to by having Peter sleep in Brooks' bed while I slept in mine pulled over against the door. But I was sure, as I had been when we were in the car in town, that Peter would not try to leave us.

The next afternoon, I watched an unbroken line of snow banks tinted purple by the windows of the limousine in which we whirred silently along the Massachusetts Turnpike towards McLean hospital in Belmont two and a half hours away. Because he felt that he and I were both too tense and short of sleep to drive at night on the return trip, Brooks had called the same taxi service which had brought Peter back from Ithaca. They had sent their biggest car. Brooks sat in front while Peter and I sat deep in the plush back seat, the jump seats folded in front of us, and passed some of the time on word scrambles from the newspaper.

In the late afternoon as we waited for the admissions procedure to begin, Peter stood in the middle of the small reception room shifting his weight from side to side. I said, "This reminds me of the day we took you to camp. You were such a lonely little boy."

He answered, "And now I'm a lonely big boy." Then just as we were called into the office, in a more urgent voice, he said, "I don't want them to change me."

Weeks later Peter would tell us that by taking action we had done what he wanted us to do. He would also tell us that on the day before we took him to Dr. Linder, his panic at the first meeting of a self-paced math class, had sent him to the roof of a department store. When he decided not to jump, he called home. I remembered the call. He had said only that he was all right but thought I might be worried because he was late.

Peter called several times a day on Saturday and Sunday, in despair at where he had ended up. We took turns talking to him and never left the house together. Tom was home on a long-planned weekend with a friend. He hadn't invited anyone home from Westminster before, and we had not wanted to cancel his weekend at the last minute. He was embarrassed by the phone calls but tried to hide his distress and entertain his friend until they left on Sunday afternoon.

Peter's calls continued on Monday and Tuesday. He was agitated by the behavior of some of the other patients. In particular he described a girl who stood right outside the booth girating and making lewd gestures at him while he was on the phone.

On Wednesday Brooks and I arrived at eleven o'clock in the morning for our first appointment at McLean's. Someone led us from the reception building to the one in which Peter lived; then left us as a staff member on his hall unlocked a heavy door. Inside, the hall had the gray, narrow look of a nineteenth-century institution. We were taken to a small conference room where we sat down around an oval table with Dr. Ely, a resident and the head of Peter's psychiatric team; Mrs. Alia, a social worker; and Peter. Dr. Ely was a thin, young woman with a very soft voice. After a few moments of silence she started. "You did the right thing in bringing him here. In six or seven weeks, we will have a work-up conference and then we will meet with you to discuss Peter's program. You will come once a week for family therapy with your social worker, Mrs. Alia. Our parents group meets on Tuesday evenings."

The words seemed to flee back into her mouth, leaving nothing in the air for discussion.

I interjected. "We live more than two hours away and I have a teaching job."

More silence. Mrs. Alia's face was round and soft. Her eyes looked sad for us. She did not look at Dr. Ely. We discovered later that she was still in training. Nearby, a door was being banged hard and deliberately as a woman screamed in accompaniment. She was in an area across the hall which we had seen the first day. There was no furniture in it, just padding on the floor and walls.

Peter looked up from where he sat quietly across from us. He looked at his father, then at me and said, "It's ironic that I've ended up in a worse situation than the colleges I ran away from." After the meeting, as Peter was not allowed to leave the unit, we sat in a small cafeteria with him while he ate lunch. We could hardly hear each other over the noise of an industrial-strength vacuum cleaner.

Peter said the staff was kind and he didn't want to cause them trouble or bring any attention to himself among his fellow patients. Not only was the unit locked but things like matches and everything in a category known as "sharps" was restricted. On a later visit, Peter would list for us some of the unlikely things people tried to swallow.

After Peter ate, he showed us his room. In spite of the gloom, his roommate's side looked as though it were at Westminster with banners, posters and photographs. The boy had been there about a year and a half. Peter said, "Mom, he's tried just about everything already and he's only fourteen."

In an alcove about halfway down the hall, the staff, young men and women with various designations on their chests, tended what looked like a hotel desk with slots and books to sign. Peter asked one of them to let us out.

We emerged from the rugged, dark stone building which hunkered in against a snowy slope and passed the white portico of the reception building where we had started with Peter the week before. In bright daylight, I was aware for the first time of the vastness of the grounds and the century of New England trees and architecture—one view was a college campus, and the next a Victorian prison.

The parking areas were flat spaces strung in front of the reception building; then the slope continued across a wide, central space to some elegant, red brick Georgian buildings. Behind us a path passed a low frame structure and wound towards a foot bridge which led to steep steps down to a quadrangle of the oldest brownstone buildings. Thereafter, we would meet Mrs. Alia in one of these, and there would be no more screams.

As we threaded through the parking lots towards our car, I looked up and saw tears on Brooks' long, craggy cheek. We talked a long time over our sandwiches at a Howard Johnson's on the pike, neither of us at all sure we had done the right thing. We felt trapped, unwilling to bring Peter home to the despair he'd been living in, but scared that he could languish for months in the labyrinthine system of McLean Hospital. I had received bland assurances from the business office that two months ($28,000), the amount of time covered by our standard health insurance policy, was an average stay. But Peter had just told us that everyone on his hall had been in residence at least six months and some, like his roommate, for eighteen.

Peter had also told us that he had heard that he could apply to be released, a process that could take two or three weeks. We did not discourage him from finding out what his rights were; he had, after all, signed himself in. For the next couple of days his voice on the phone sounded unhappy but less agitated.

Then on Saturday evening, only eight days after his arrival at McLean's, Peter suddenly said to Brooks, " You know, Dad, I think I can get something out of this place."

A few days later, he wrote to Carolyn in Ireland.

> Dear Carolyn,
>
> Things aren't too great here. I know I have to learn to deal with people, but this isn't the easiest place to do it. But anyway, I have to give it some time.
>
> I hope things are going well for you in your new location. It sounded like it was going to be a lot more comfortable. It was great to see you over the holidays. I feel like I acted out of it around you and I hope you didn't take it the wrong way. It's just that I knew I had to get going in some direction but I didn't want to think about it, so instead I kind of "shut down."
>
> That's pretty much why I'm in this place.
>
> On to your problems, how about courses? How many this term, ten, twelve? In addition, how's the pub life? Does it still consume a good 2/3 of your day? What about cigarettes? The longer you smoke...sound familiar?
>
> <u>New Topic</u>
>
> If you're going to go into social work, prepare yourself

for abuse. I see it here every day. It's only verbal abuse but it must be demoralizing.

Lastly

Say hello to Liz for me. Good luck, and I love you.

Love, Peter

Before we started the weekly family therapy sessions with Mrs. Alia, which were to include Peter, Brooks and I each made a separate trip to give her information about our respective families. Brooks told of his older brother's schizophrenia, largely untreated and not diagnosed until his middle age, and of his father's two hospitalizations for depression when he was in his late thirties. In my family, my maternal grandfather's depressive cycles had dominated his middle age (he died of cancer at fifty-seven), while my mother's depressions had started when she was about sixty. Neither was ever hospitalized but my mother had been responding well to lithium therapy for almost twenty years. All this information went into Peter's file, full of inaccuracies but with the general gist intact. None of it would ever be discussed in any of our meetings with hospital staff.

As Mrs. Alia was our only scheduled contact with the hospital and our phone calls to Dr. Ely elicited only assurances that Peter was well placed and well cared for, after three weeks, we began to envision that a month hence, at the promised seventh week evaluation meeting, Dr. Ely would tell us that Peter should stay at the hospital for several months longer. Knowing this would require financial resources beyond our income and feeling that we desperately needed more information from those working with Peter, we decided to try to circumvent Dr. Ely. We discovered that an acquaintance knew a member of the hospital's board of trustees, and through him we made known our desire to talk to a doctor senior to Dr. Ely. As a result of this maneuver I received a call from the doctor who would be designated as Psychiatrist-in-Charge on all the documents in Peter's file. This man briefly discussed some diagnostic possibilities with me, saying they thought Peter might have a borderline personality disorder, but I could get no sense from our conversation of how long he expected him to be in the hospital. I would not have another chance to talk him.

However, grasping at the new term I had been fed, I found a title and ordered a book about borderline personality disorders. A defintion of the disorder was elusive but the book outlined case histories of young men who acted out their angers and were unable to make friends. None of their behaviors sounded remotely like Peter's.

When Brooks went to McLean's the next day for his conference with Mrs. Alia, Dr. Ely appeared to say that we had caused nothing but trouble by calling a trustee. Brooks stood his ground reasserting our need to know more about Peter's treatment. Unfortunately the laws protecting Peter's privacy were on Dr. Ely's side and our efforts proved useless.

A few days after this encounter Peter called to say that an aftercare nurse had encouraged him to put his name down for a psychiatric halfway house in Boston, which was run by McLean's. Peter had begun to relax as he became accustomed to the routines and was allowed to leave his hall more often, but he was anxious at the prospects of a further change. We were initially surprised at the timing of the suggestion, but told him that just putting his name down could do no harm. We soon came to understand, that the nurse was following the standard routine of planning ahead for a patient whose insurance would end in four or five weeks. The options were for Peter to return home and continue with outpatient therapy, transfer to a state institution or, if the family could afford it and a bed were available, to spend time at a halfway house, costing about $2,000 a month. Mrs. Alia brought the subject up as she and I walked together leaving one of our family meetings. She reminded me of the date on which our insurance would run out and assumed that we would want to discuss with her the options for Peter's future.

Dr. Ely, however, made a different assumption. "By the middle of February, both the patient and his parents had pressured members of the treatment team to explore possibilities for alternative placement," she would write in her summary of Peter's hospital stay.

By the time the subject of the halfway house was presented to him, Peter already had another source of support. He had been assigned for individual therapy, to a Dr. Rhodes, one of the many psychiatrists who have their offices at McLean's. These doctors are not members of the in-hospital staff but confer with them when their patients are in residence. While he was in the hospital Peter met with Dr. Rhodes three times a week and after he was discharged, would continue therapy on a less frequent basis for another nineteen months.

I remember clearly our sense of hope when Peter first told us of Dr. Rhodes. He said he liked him, something he had never said about Dr. Linder. He felt, almost immediately, that he was making progress in understanding himself and what had happened to him. Encouraged by such remarks and by the buoyancy in Peter's step as he hurried across the quadrangle to meet us for family therapy sessions, we lost some of our zeal in penetrating Dr. Ely's reserve.

Ironically another sign that Peter was returning to normal was his ability to be humorous about Dr. Ely. One week, as Brooks drove us to the Friendly's in Belmont, Peter turned from the front seat to give me the full benefit of his imitation of Dr. Ely's frustration at a Monday hall meeting, where no one could dredge up a weekend trauma of sufficient magnitude for her.

However, Dr. Ely was the head of Peter's psychiatric team and he was wary of the fact that as such she had power over his future. He wanted to go back to college in the fall, and he reported to Dr. Rhodes and to us that Dr. Ely had told him he wouldn't be ready for that and had not been willing to assign him help in getting applications out. Apparently, Dr. Rhodes felt Peter was giving up too easily in the face of Dr. Ely's comments and encouraged him to further discussion with her. Peter, in turn, told Dr. Rhodes that he saw Dr. Ely as fragile and overburdened and did not want to burden her further. Eventually he did pursue the subject with her and she reluctantly agreed to his working on applications.

In the first weeks of March, the intractable snow banks which had ushered Peter into McLean's melted away so rapidly that on the day on which we were to meet Dr. Rhodes, Peter appeared in a summer shirt as we parked on the glistening pavement outside his building. Tom was with us, because his long spring vacation had begun. Peter told Dr. Rhodes that he was annoyed with us for taking for granted that Tom's coming would be all right with him. Apparently, he did not want to appear as a patient in front of his younger brother.

Dr. Rhodes was a young man, clean shaven with neat, dark hair and dressed in good tweeds. Quiet and pleasant in manner, he had none of the intensity which might have unnerved Peter. As we sat in his office with Peter (Tom stayed in the car), I realized that for the first time we were hearing an opinion and that I could ask direct questions. We asked about the antidepressant Peter was taking. He had complained of side effects, dizziness, sweating and thirst. Dr. Rhodes told us that it was hard to attribute the dramatic improvement in Peter's mood to the medication, because his mood had lifted before a therapeutic level had been reached. And while he recommended that Peter stay on desiprimine for six months gradually lessening the dosage, he also made it clear that he did not feel the pills were an important part of Peter's therapy.

Then without prompting from us, Dr. Rhodes addressed the family histories which we had given to Mrs. Alia. I sensed that he wanted to assure Peter, in front of us, that he saw no connection between Peter's present problems and those in our families. He did not deny that Peter had had a major episode of depression, but he characterized it as a classic adolescent crisis, an inability to cope with independence. Now that Peter was no longer in a depressed state they could work, he said, on his coping skills. One of us must have interjected a question about the events which had brought Peter to McLean's. Without hesitation Dr. Rhodes said that he did not think Peter had ever been seriously suicidal.

Brooks and I both came away from the meeting with the feeling that we had heard good news.

The next week at school, a friend and colleague asked me about Peter. She had known him all his life as her son's friend and as a student, and was pleased to hear how much better he felt. Then she said in a tone that was half-question, half-statement, "And they've told him what to do it if happens again?"

I did not answer her directly. I would not have said aloud that I didn't think that whatever "it" was which had led Peter to think of suicide would happen to him again. But I felt at that time as if he had survived a dangerous disease and was therefore immunized against its most virulent forms.

On March 10 Peter's psychiatric team, including Dr. Rhodes and several of the staff who had worked with him in other capacities such as art therapy, held a work-up conference. This was the meeting Dr. Ely had told us would occur. Its purpose was to review Peter's case, his progress in the hospital and make recommendations for his future treatment. Two days later Dr. Ely and a few of the staff held a meeting with Brooks and me.

By then, our talk with Dr. Rhodes had taken the edge off of our wariness of the McLean's system, and as I entered the room and saw that Dr. Ely had a file folder on her lap, I thought that we were about to get an evaluation of Peter's condition, a diagnosis. (There was one, "Major depression-recurrent" but it was not given to us.)

In her shallow voice, Dr. Ely addressed me first. "The time of the baby's death must have been very difficult for you and your family."

I was, as must have been her intent, totally surprised by this remark, but not silenced. My mind whipped along. Thinking I must relate this to Peter, I said, "I think Tom's birth had a greater effect on Peter's life than Julie's death."

As I looked around at the doctors and staff, I had no concept of the weight which, as I would one day learn, Dr. Ely had attached to the event. My reply must have seemed evasive, and she dropped the subject and opened her folder to read off Peter's adult IQ score and report that a small lump had been seen in an x-ray of the base of his skull. A further test would be done, but they did not expect it to reveal anything of significance.

We went on to talk of Peter's projected move to the halfway house. Dr. Ely would report that anxiety and anger pervaded the meeting because a bed would be ready for Peter a week sooner than had originally been expected. I remember no anger, only that Peter was worried that he would not be able to organize a required thirty-hour-a-week schedule in time to take advantage of the available space. We agreed to pay to hold the bed for a week if he needed more time.

Finally, we were told that our family therapy was to continue after Peter left the hospital, but with another social worker as Mrs. Alia's training period would end in March. We protested saying that we had looked forward to coming on weekends to visit Peter in Boston rather than during the school week. As a practical matter, I had missed a lot of classes. But Dr. Ely said further therapy was essential, and we agreed to continue after April first on an every other week basis.

As the hour ended, Mrs. Alia thanked us for our openness in talking of our respective families. Our last meetings with her went as smoothly as the ones before. One week I went alone because Brooks took Tom to New York City to cheer up his vacation. The next week, I stayed home to attend an end-of-the-term faculty meeting while Brooks and Mrs. Alia bid each other a cordial goodbye.

My final conversation with Dr. Ely was more difficult. Suddenly in the last days of March, just as Peter was all prepared to move to Berkeley House on April first, the day on which a bed would be available to him, Dr. Ely told him she didn't think he was ready to leave the hospital for at least another week. If he did leave, she would record his departure as AMA–"against medical advise." Peter called us very distressed because he had worked to set up the required outpatient program and had visited Berkeley House several times. Brooks talked to him and told him he should be sure he felt ready to leave and not to worry about money because we had resources. Peter was well aware of the high cost of McLean's and had told us how sorry he felt for people he had seen bundled off to state hospitals when their long-term insurance ran out. We did not tell him that we had taken out a second mortgage on our house when, as soon as our insurance ended, the business office had asked for two-weeks' hospital costs in advance, the first month's $2,000 payment for the halfway house and $1,800 to be put in escrow for a total of $11,000. For the moment, Dr. Ely was asking Peter to stay in the hospital for exactly the amount of time for which we had already paid. Peter had hoped some of this money could go toward Berkeley House, but now he just wanted us to call Dr. Ely to forestall any further delays.

I called and told her I thought Peter was very disappointed not to be allowed to make a move he had so carefully prepared for. She said he needed more time to say goodbye. Then, the following exchange was repeated several times.

Dr. Ely: I think there is something we are not saying.

Me: There is nothing I am not saying, Dr. Ely, but if there is something you are not saying, please tell me what it is.

Dr. Ely: (After a long pause.) I think there is something we are not saying.

Brooks was gesturing to me, mouthing that I should try to end the call without offending Dr. Ely. Somehow, I did.

We held our breaths for the first week of April, and then Dr. Ely signed Peter's release. He moved into Berkeley House without our help and immediately was glad to be there. There was a balcony outside his room and soon after he moved a magnolia tree was in bloom below his window. Peter called to say he'd been sitting in the sun watching the world go by.

I had a week off from school towards the end of April

and Brooks and I spent a day in northwestern Connecticut wandering around the country roads of his childhood before we went on to Boston for a visit with Peter and an introduction to the director of the half-way house.

Berkeley House is an old brownstone "two blocks over and one block down from the Ritz" as Peter wrote to Carolyn, adding, "I'll probably never have such a good address in Boston again." A half-glassed door at the top of the front steps led to a dark hall where we sat on a stiff old fashioned sofa waiting for our appointment.

The director confirmed what Peter had told us; he was adjusting very well, was perhaps a little euphoric, but that would pass. He expected that Peter would be able to move into an apartment or college dormitory after about six months. Others like Peter had done this successfully; he cited examples. We left feeling grateful to the aftercare nurse at McLean's who had encouraged Peter to put his name down for a bed in Berkeley House.

Peter was halfway and moving determinedly from the world of the hospital towards that of the city, his friends and eventually college. He called up Jeff and told him very honestly what had happened to him. Then he began to meet with Jeff and others of their Westminster friends who were in Boston.

Aware that his high mood would not last, Peter followed a prescription which he and Dr. Rhodes had worked out, walking himself through each new endeavor before he was actually due to start on it. He prepared himself in this way for a summer course at the Boston Harbor campus of the University of Massachusetts, and then for a part-time job scooping ice cream at a Haagen-Daz store a few blocks from Berkeley House. As he took on these new pursuits, Peter gradually dropped the activities and group therapy sessions he had been attending at McLean's. The group was getting annoyed by his cheerfulness anyway, he told us.

While he was greatly relieved to find that he could rejoin the normal world, Peter did not want to deny that he had been hospitalized for depression. So when he went to get his driver's license renewed, he checked the "yes" box for the question on mental illness. At that point, as he told it, bells rang, people scurried around, and he was ushered to an upstairs room. After some delay, someone was found who could handle the situation and he was interviewed and given his license.

Peter was still going out to McLean's twice a week to meet with Dr. Rhodes and every other week, he joined us there for family therapy with our new social worker. As both the hospital and the University's Boston Harbor campus are a long subway ride from the center of the city, he spent a great deal of time on the T.

After a late June appointment, we had our usual lunch with Peter and discussed the increasing difficulty of arranging these family meetings. We decided to stop the therapy. Peter warned us that the social worker would pressure us to continue, and encouraged us to be firm. He had learned that it was important to exercise one's own judgement at a place like McLean's. He looked at us across the narrow booth at the Friendly's in Belmont, and said, "I think I had to crash and burn."

I finished the image to myself. He was rising like the phoenix.

9

By the fall Peter would be enrolled as a fulltime student at the University of Massachusetts in Boston. In one of the boxes of papers from his desk I found an essay he wrote for his English class that term. The subject was stereotyping and he told me at the time,that he had used as his example the stigma attached to patients in mental hospitals. His illustration, based on his experiences at McLean's, ends with the sentence, "Lastly, I learned that going to a psychiatric hospital is not the end of the world. It was the beginning of mine."

It seemed to Brooks and me that McLean's and later Berkeley House had given Peter a ladder, a way up and out of a situation he had seen as hopeless. In our relief we found it easy to slough off our frustrations at having been caught in a system that had treated us more as patients than parents. It did not occur to me that as a result of this approach we might have been denied opinions and even warnings about what could happen to Peter in the future.

I made my first request to McLean's for Peter's records about two months after his death at the time that Tom went back to Westminster for his final term. His immediate call to tell me of a college acceptance letter that had been waiting in his mailbox led me to thinking about Peter's return to school in the spring of his senior year and I wrote in my journal, "It was then that the troubles which led to his suicide could be said to have started." As I began to sketch in the events of his last three and a half years, the tight hold that Peter's January voice had held in my mind loosened for a little while. I realized that I needed to work my way through the maze which Peter had walked especially after he left Ithaca. I wanted to talk to some of the people he had talked to, to read what he had said to them and what they had said about him.

I had no idea that the paper trail on which I was about to start would continue for two years nor did I bargain on the amount of description I would find of Brooks and myself. However, I realized there might be some derogatory remarks when I received my first reply from McLean's. A doctor with the enigmatic title, Director Quality Assurance, wrote that, "After careful consideration by Peter's McLean staff and myself, it was agreed that it would not be in your best interests to have the record."

This premise I knew was false. The staff at McLean's were no more willing to discuss Peter's death with me than they had been his life, but at the time I did not, as they must have presumed, have either the energy or the knowledge of my legal rights with which to persist. The letter went on to say that they had agreed to send a portion of the file to a therapist whom I had begun to see and who had already made contact with Dr. Rhodes. When this file arrived my doctor read it to me verbatim thereby breaking the commandments stenciled in large red letters on the envelope.

Speculations about Peter's condition were made in terms like dependent, avoidant, paranoid, even schizoid and the phrase I had heard from the head of Peter's unit, borderline personality disorder. My therapist said the last two were catchall terms used for a variety of behaviors. There was one sentence I asked him to repeat because it stated that Peter was not subject to impulsive behavior, not subject to panic.

I began to haunt local bookstores and libraries looking

for information on anxiety, depression and suicide. There was almost nothing on the shelves but as soon as I found a book I began to trace others going from one bibliography to the next, ordering them from the bookstore in town or on interlibrary loan.

As I handed over the scraps of paper with titles on them to one of the librarians or to the bookstore owner, all of whom knew me, I sensed their distress at my requests, their hopes that soon I would order something on another subject. Whenever one of them called, I immediately drove into town to pick up whatever book had arrived. I could not resist skimming the pages in the car before I returned home to start reading, often to be disgusted by the categories into which suicides are herded by some statisticians, the addicted, the socially deviant, the criminally insane. In more enlightened texts Peter might appear in a sentence or two only to disappear as my eyes swallowed whole paragraphs of behaviors quite unlike anything he had ever done.

Brooks and the children referred to my reading matter as "those books." "Did you get that from one of those books?" would often be the response to one of my observations about Peter. It seemed to them that in my total preoccupation with his death I was arrogating Peter entirely to myself, acting as if, as they said, there had been no one in the family except him and me. But when, in the fall of 1989, I decided to renew and expand my quest for Peter's records, they did not try to stop me. Eventually they would come to view the long process with a mixture of forbearance and curiosity as I sent for, argued for, sought consultations about and immersed myself in the records of Peter's last years.

The Berkshire Mental Health Center which had taken Peter into their crisis house right after he returned from Ithaca and a few months later secured a place for him at McLean's, agreed to release their files to me if I would come in person to sign for them. While a machine ground out copies of the pages, I waited in an area familiar to me from the snowy day we sat there with Peter, the day on which they advised us to take him to McLean's. When the secretary handed me the still warm papers, I leafed through them quickly and saw that the last page contained a letter from McLean's to the man who had arranged Peter's hospitalization. The writer thanked him for sending Peter to them and closed by saying, "I hope you will feel free to communicate should you have any questions or information for us."

Riffling back I saw that the other pages contained direct clinical observations on Peter's behavior at a time when thoughts of suicide had first become a threat to him. The notes were handwritten in scripts that changed as the eight-hour duty shifts had in the low, brown shingle house, where many people took turns watching over Peter for five days.

The person on duty when Peter arrived wrote, "He is thinking of suicide with a plan of jumping out a window." The next day, Peter was quoted as saying, "I don't really want to kill myself." But later in his stay, he tells a staff member that he knows he will eventually have to kill himself, that he feels no love for Brooks and me, that he feels as though he has abandoned us, that he doesn't feel anything.

Each of his watchers described Peter's tremendous fear and noted that he responded well to an anti-anxiety medication. Yet on the day Peter left for the hospital the person on the afternoon shift wrote only, "Client's Ativan left in med. cabinet."

"Was this file ever sent on to anyone else?" I asked the uneasy messenger.

She hesitated. "You'll find it indicated in there if it was." There was nothing to that effect.

For more than two years, while Peter was hospitalized and in extended therapy first in Pittsfield and then in Boston, these reports sat securely in an office drawer. It would have taken only Peter's signature to make them available to any of the professionals or institutions into whose care he was subsequently delivered.

These descriptions did not even accompany Peter to the Berkshire Medical Center, the hopital a few streets away where he spent the next twelve days. This institution readily mailed me their records and I found on the first page a difference of perception which I realized had influenced Peter's initial course of treatment.

The counsellor-in-training who interviewed Peter on admission characterized his state as one of "major depression," while a few hours later Dr. Donald, the head psychiatrist, noted a touch of humor in Peter's responses and concluded that his problems were no more than "an adjustment disorder." It was based on this second opinion that we were told that Peter did not need any medication and that he was sent on to Dr. Linder.

I had had no contact with Dr. Linder since the morning of Peter's suicidal crisis when he had passed us on to the Berkshire Mental Health Center. But when I wrote in the late fall to ask for his notes he sent them immediately and offered to talk to me. I accepted his offer and soon found myself in some of the same dingy hallways through which we had followed Peter almost three years before. I was grateful that Dr. Linder, at least, had moved to another office space.

He opened the waiting room door to usher me into the office and as we sat down, I prepared myself to respond to his condolences only to be completely numbed by his first words. "What is your Blue Cross number?" he asked. Not to be deterred at that point, I quickly took out a check, made it out for the price of one session and handed it to him. He took the check and we proceeded. He had wondered why Peter had not returned to his care and was relieved to hear that he had moved to Boston after leaving McLean's. Depression, he went on to tell me, didn't worry him; he had never lost a patient; psychiatric drugs were not his responsibility. When the hour was up I thanked him for his time, but a few days later wrote to tell him of my distress at his complacence.

My therapist supported my second request for information from McLean's in a letter in which he expressed the opinion that nothing the staff had said could make me feel any more responsible for Peter's death than I already did. Our letters elicited only a small portion of the file, Dr. Ely's fifteen-page Discharge Summary of Peter's time under her care.

Of Brooks' and my efforts to consult with another doctor at McLean's, Dr. Ely had written, "This action was interpreted as narcissistic entitlement and anxiety over the pathology in their own families and in their son." I asked my doctor how he would interpret this assessment and he answered, "She was your enemy." When he had read her whole report he told me he didn't think there was any way we could have gotten around Dr. Ely without causing Peter more distress. She controlled all his so-called privileges starting with that of leaving his unit.

Dr. Rhodes, on the other hand, had appeared as an ally both to Peter and to us. But now I needed to understand how he had come to his sanguine view of Peter's condition, how he had assessed Peter's suicidal gestures and what records he had seen before starting to work with him. Several people in the mental health profession told me that I could not expect to gain access to Dr. Rhodes' notes on his treatment of Peter so I was not surprised when my first letter to him went unanswered for two months. I sent a second letter by registered mail and this elicited a call. Dr. Rhodes could not answer my questions on the phone and was not willing to send his notes but said he would refer to them and address in writing the questions I had posed in my letters and reiterated on the phone. In the course of a long conversation he suggested that Peter's desire to get out of McLean's was too precipitous, behavior that therapists called "a flight to health." I had thought that Dr. Rhodes had been one of those encouraging Peter in this so-called flight, but I didn't say anything in order not to jeopardize my chances of getting further information.

When, after two months, I had heard nothing, I sent another registered letter to say that if I could not get answers in any other way, I would seek legal help. Almost immediately Dr. Rhodes called to say that he had been about to write me when he received my threats. He offered me an appointment to talk but I declined, sure that, unless I had the records in front of me, he could as easily parry my questions in person as he had on the phone.

The first lawyer I consulted said he thought I would have to sue Dr. Rhodes in order to get access to his files. When I eventually decided to look into this possibility the lawyer refered me to a colleague who advised me to call the Massachusetts Board of Health in Boston. The problem was suddenly resolved when, from a lawyer there, I learned that the piece of paper which had designated Brooks as the executor to Peter's estate, i.e., his bank account, gave him the legal access to all of his possessions, psychological records included.

Most of the pages in Dr. Rhodes thick file on Peter were handwritten and it took me a while to figure out the meanings of the symbols and arrows and of his use of parentheses. The latter appeared to indicate his thinking rather than Peter's. The first pages contained a brief recapitulation of what Dr. Rhodes had read in the admission report. The story of Peter's abortive attempts to start college ended with, "Ithaca College-fall '86—-again very anxious, 'too much independence,' mother resisted his wish to leave, led to 'device' of suicidality."

A few weeks into their sessions Dr. Rhodes led Peter to describe how he had felt just before coming to McLean's.

> 3/2/87–Events of several days prior to admit: parents requested (required?) him to take courses. Went through motions with sense he'll find a way out—won't have to do it. Increase of suicide thoughts as course demands grow. One day signed for self-paced math course, 'epitome of what I can't possibly do'—went to store building 7th floor. Felt much calmer with idea he could just jump—equals a way out of responsibilities/obligations/expectations(and others' anger/disappointment with him?)
>
> 3/4/87–Night preceding suicidal day couldn't sleep—worrying about how to avoid school responsibility the next day. Saw he couldn't help self, so what is way out? Next morning told parents he saw 'visions' in night, result went to Dr.

> Linder, told him of 'visions'—not true—and of suicidality, how he'd gone to top of building, etc. Led to McLean referral.

These were the only conversations Dr. Rhodes recorded on the subject of Peter's suicidal feelings. In the following weeks he supported Peter in his effort to confront Dr. Ely on the subject of her reservations about his scheduled discharge.

The concluding words for the day on which Brooks and I had met with Dr. Rhodes jibed with my memory: "A clinical depression due to maturational/ developmental crisis in personality development and growing up. Doesn't have an illness as such." It was in this vein that he had told us that he did not think that Peter had ever been seriously suicidal. And I, whom everyone including Peter dubbed as the family worrier, the skeptic, the pessimist, had accepted this opinion, allowing myself to forget that Dr. Rhodes had never seen the Peter who paced the emergency room with a tingling face or heard the Peter who circled our living room saying that suicide was the only solution for him.

By the time Peter arrived at McLean's his second suicidal crisis had passed and the doctors and staff had seen only the agitation of its aftermath. Brooks and I were the only ones who had lived with Peter through his five months of acute and recurring suicidal crises, but we were only allowed to report on ourselves and never on Peter's behavior in these months.

After I had studied Dr. Rhodes' notes I typed up the handwritten pages in order to give them to a Boston psychologist, who had done some research on suicide. He agreed to take me on as a client for the express purpose of reviewing Peter's records and soon after we started to meet he suggested that I ought have a complete file from McLean's. I obtained the full two hundred pages after sending the hospital a copy of the document which had made Brooks executor of Peter's estate.

Peter had been dead for two years by the time I read the details of his daily life at McLean's as well as transcripts of meetings his psychiatric team held among themselves and those the social worker held with Brooks and me. I was not surprised to read that Peter had been well-behaved and considerate of others at all times nor that he had resisted joining his fellow patients in purely social situations. The lifting of his mood within two weeks of his arrival was noted and when the reasons for his hospitalization, his suicidal "ideation and gestures," were listed, they were explained as bids for attention that he had not been able to get in any other way.

So had started the search for the causes of Peter's mental state. It ended with a classic tracing of adult neuroses to a childhood trauma, in his case a situation of early abandonment which had never occured. I found the tale summarized by Mrs. Alia in a transcript of the "work-up" conference held by Peter's treatment team two days before their meeting with Brooks and me.

> Mrs. Alia: At two and a half years of age [sic] his infant sister died. This would seem to be a sentinel event in his life. Peter was sent to live with his grandmother in Brookline…His mother became quite depressed but neither her depression nor the infant's death was discussed among family members.

In another place Mrs. Alia specified that Peter had spent a year with my mother at this time. Peter had reported memories of his grandmother bathing and dressing him, but nowhere was it made clear that these memories came from the ten days that he had spent with my mother at the time of Julie's birth and that he had not been sent to stay with her after Julie died.

In their search for a psychiatrically sound basis for Peter's condition, a number of the staff had allowed these inaccuracies of fact to feed their supositions and, ultimately, to escalate into conclusions without further reference to the people involved. It seemed as though Peter, Brooks and I had been lost in a text book.

However, Mrs. Alia's confusion over the events following the baby's death seemed more explicable than the statements she made about Brooks and me in her summation of the half dozen, one hour family therapy sessions she had held with us and Peter. She was a young woman, still in training, who spoke with a strong foreign accent and I remember wondering, at the time, how much she could understand of our unremittingly Yankee backgrounds. There is nothing in her brief notes on these meetings to indicate how she came to her conclusions.

> Mrs. Alia: The family is extremely rigid and anxious around Peter and has a great deal of expectations from him and then deny that they have these. The parents have considerable marital difficulties and are unable to look at these problems. There are a number of secrets in the family and all members have major difficulties expressing their anger.

Later in the transcript a statement by Dr. Ely also assumes that there are family secrets. I now realize that her question about the loss of my baby, that had so startled me on the day when I sat among the staff expecting to hear an assessment of Peter's condition, was her way of flushing out what she believed to be an important secret. It follows that since Brooks and I had appeared to have been secretive about this event, she concluded that we must also have been hiding other family upheavals.

Mrs. Alia's assumption that we all had problems with anger may well have been based on comments made about Peter by others on the staff, who wrote that he equated expressing strong emotions with loss of control. Towards the end of the meeting a senior doctor picked up on this theme and made the only statement in the transcript which described Peter's suicidal behavior as something more than a need for attention, as behavior which could be seen as a prediction of future risk for him. Her comments were based on a single interview with Peter of which he told Dr. Rhodes, "She got it all."

> Dr. B.…He was extremely frightened when entering college; the dormitory life he saw as an orgiastic environment,

> wild and sexual, where students were out of control. This degree of anxiety leaves him feeling as though it is impossible to feel in control. He often feels out of control. His interest in suicide seems to have been an obsession where he could think of nothing else.

The meeting was drawing to a close and this warning about the consequences of Peter's acute anxiety was lost among recommendations for his future treatment including his move to the halfway house. The psychiatrist-in-charge, to whom I had spoken when we tried to circumvent Dr. Ely for information, concluded that, "the major work to be done with Peter is that of separating from his family." Then he speculated that a critical time for Peter might come in September if he returned to school.

10

THE DOCTOR AT MCLEAN'S NEED NOT HAVE WORRIED ABOUT Peter's separation from Brooks and me. While, in the past, avoidance for Peter had often meant coming or staying home, his months of depression had twisted the situation around until he feared home as a place that could trap him into a state of lethargy and helplessness.

With the approval of our second family therapist Brooks and I suggested that Peter try coming back to Lenox for just a weekend in June to celebrate our twenty-fifth anniversary. Peter agreed and on a Friday he and Brooks drove to the airport to meet Carolyn's plane from Ireland and then came on home. The next evening before the three children took us to a restaurant for dinner, Carolyn took some pictures one of which was of Peter sitting on the front steps. In the fall she would have it enlarged and put it in a frame as a birthday present for me. Peter reported to Dr. Rhodes that the weekend had been easier than he had expected and he ventured a five day stay when his summer school classes ended in August.

On that visit he kept himself busy playing tennis and golf with Tom and a couple of times made evening dates with local friends. His greatest social challenge was an invitation to the twenty-first birthday party of a childhood friend with whom he had not had much recent contact. The boy was at Harvard rowing on a winning crew, his college life the epitome of what Peter had seen as out of his reach. Peter planned his moves carefully; he did not want to arrive too early and he did not want to drink too much. He also wanted to be honest with friends about how he had spent the past year. He managed all these objectives and said the next day, "It was hard, but I'm glad I did it."

Peter returned to the security of Berkeley House and the relative security of the U Mass Boston Harbor campus. The locale was familiar to him from the summer but he later wrote that he had made only "a few forays into social interaction" as he described "the hordes of people of all ages teeming through the halls, bobbing heads, trained eyes, pistoning arms, loud conversations." He would soon decide that staying at U. Mass would constitute an excuse for not meeting people and challenged himself to apply for transfer to Boston University's School of Communications for the following academic year.

Once he was sure that he could handle his routine at U. Mass. Peter became determined to prove that he no longer needed to be in a halfway house. In mid-November he started living in an apartment with four girls none of whom he had met until just before he moved in. It semed a situation guaranteed to make him uncomfortable, but he had not had any luck finding a place where he could share the rent, until Jeff told him of these girls who lived in a large apartment and had a spare room. One of them was Wendy, a friend of a friend of Jeff's sister.

The apartment was in Allston in an area of solidly built apartment buildings with large rooms, many of them full of students and in disrepair. On the day we helped Peter move in, I embarrassed him by expressing concern about the gaping holes in the walls of the hallway and the broken lock on one of the entry doors. Peter's room was at the back overlooking an alley in which fights sometimes took place. The area made him nervous, but he was amazed at how quickly he became accustomed to dealing with or ignoring the difficult behavior of two of the girls. This was due in part to the fact that Wendy immediately became his friend and they dealt with the problems of the menage together.

Then in April Peter and Wendy escaped to a smaller, better kept apartment on Commonwealth Avenue also in Allston. Brooks made a trip to Boston to see the new apartment and co-sign the lease. It was drawn up for sixteen months, a length of time which inspired Peter to improve his furnishings. He replaced a roll-away bed borrowed from Carolyn with a new queen size one and a card table, Brooks had bought him for the first apartment, with the desk from his room at home.

On April 25, Peter and Brooks loaded this desk into our station wagon and drove it to Boston. Peter had come home the night before because he was due to appear in court that Monday morning in the neighboring town of Lee. The incident which necessitated this appearance had occured a month earlier when Peter, home for spring vacation, had passed a school bus while driving through Lenox engrossed in an argument with Tom. The outcome of the case provided Peter with a captivating opening for the journal he started that evening.

> *April 25, 1988: I now have a criminal record, which in and of itself is an intriguing fact. However, the reality of passing a school bus before coming to a full stop is hardly glamorous. Nevertheless, from here on in when completing a job application, I will be obliged to answer yes to the question of whether I've ever been convicted of a criminal offense. This seems fair to me. But I cannot deny a somewhat twisted sense of embarrassment concerning my crime. Carrying around a reputation as a bus passer is not going to intimidate many people. Granted, what I did could have resulted in the death of another person. But if I shun reason and coddle my vanity, then I can't help feeling inadequate to the task of toting around a genuine criminal record. At the very least, I should have committed some minor theft to earn my record, something indicating a premed-*

itated approach to breaking the law.

In fact, I felt a bizarre sense of envy as I sat in the courtroom listening to my fellow offenders being offered continuances because their offenses required a jury trial. When I stood up to take the rap, it was very cut and dried.

Judge:The state does not deem this offence serious enough to appoint you counsel. Will you seek outside counsel?

Peter:No, I would like to take care of this today.

From a practical perspective, I did want to get it done with. But it would have been kind of fun to announce vehemently that I did indeed plan to seek counsel, and that I would pursue justice to the highest court in the land, if I had to.

All flights of fancy aside, I really had no choice since justice was being served. But that didn't make it any easier to stomach the fact that I have a criminal record because I was more intent upon arguing with my passenger than I was in watching the road.

But I can take solace in the fact that in court that day there was a young man careless enough to drive with an expired license. He only got fined $50 which pales in comparison to my debt to society of $115.

The idea of keeping a journal had come from the woman who was to be Peter's instructor in a writing seminar at Oxford University in the coming summer. Peter wrote in longhand on sheets of standard size paper using every other line so he could change and add words easily. Whenever I read it I can hear Peter's voice saying some of the phrases, especially the throwaway ones with which he could succinctly sum up his thoughts or a situation.

After describing his court appearance Peter turned to more mundane aspects of his life, like the hours he spent in the stations and on the cars of the Massachusetts Transit Authority. Two different lines were required for each of his regular destinations, college, his job at a delicatessen and Dr. Rhodes' office at McLean's. It was a cold wet spring which as Peter wrote "carries a fair amount of clout with my day to day mood." He had two colds, couldn't get on the golf links and the Red Sox got rained out five times.

April 26, 1988: While waiting for the T train, I saw a man walking on the tracks. His eyes were carefully covering every inch of ground before him.

As he passed me, he leaned down slowly, grabbed a soda can and placed it in a trash bag he was carrying. I instantly decided he was a derelict, hoping to turn in enough cans to buy his next meal or next bottle or cigarettes or whatever.

It was getting cold as I waited for the train and I felt anger toward this presumed derelict. There was nothing tangible about my anger. If I had been in the mood, I could have thought of a hundred ways society had "screwed over" this poor guy, and I probably could have felt sorry for him. But I didn't. I was mad at him for looking the way he looked. It was an unsatisfying anger but it was easier than getting mad at myself; mad at myself for not dressing warmly enough, for forgetting to buy soap, for losing my T-pass, for any number of things.

My anger subsided as I saw the distant headlight of the oncoming train. Before the train arrived, the same man walked by me on the platform. This time, he was sweeping debris into a dustpan. I felt warmer now, and the derelict had a job.

April 30, 1988: I haven't made it to a baseball game this year. But I got a feeling of what I was missing from listening to a group of young boys talking on the subway.

They were on their way to a game. There were four of them clustered by the steps of the car. The boys were with adults who seemed to be on the "outs," except when one of the youngsters posed a question.

The whole group had boarded the subway at North Station. The train was in the middle of a delay between Worth Street and Hay Market, when the boy nearest me tossed back his head and said,

"How many stops do we have to go, Dad?"

The father was speaking to another man, and, without looking in his son's direction, replied,

"Oh, about six, uh, five, yeah six, that's it."

It's seven stops, I thought to myself. But judging by the downtrodden reaction of the boy and his friends, I thought it best to leave it at six.

The boys quickly seemed to resign themselves to the length of the trip and resolutely moved on to new topics. The youngest or at least smallest among the group, pointing with a stubby finger to the pitch blackness outside our subway, asked no one in particular,

"What would you do if you saw a hundred dollar bill lying out there?"

This question elicited numerous responses from the three other boys.

I loved the question. It wasn't a five-year-old's question. It was the question of somebody going to a ball game.

May 14, 1988: Woke up this morning to a tortuous earache. It lasted for two solid hours. Nothing I did relieved the pain, aside from short dozes. During the dozes, I even dreamt I had an earache. I've definitely had more enjoyable Saturday mornings. Still, I managed to learn something from the ordeal. What I learned concerns the nature of physical pain; specifically, its ability to unite the psyche.

Typically, when I first wake up every morning, my collective psyche seems to be pleased that there is still a world and it's still part of it. However, it doesn't take long for my psyche to tackle the tasks of the day. There is nothing wrong with this. The problem lies in my psyche's methods for facing these demands. Often, it will ignore my physical limitations concerning being in two places at the same time. The result is that many times prior to even getting out of bed, my psyche has scattered itself from whether I have any clean socks, to whether I have enough money to cover the rent, and all issues great and small in between.

This morning was different, though. All I could think of was how to ease the pain. For my psyche, it was a very satisfying situation. It had a break from all the other toils of the upcoming day. None of those mattered until the pain was gone. This total assimilation of mind and body is a state I would like to achieve more often, and sans the catalyst of intense pain.

Peter recovered enough that weekend to call and tell his father that he had bought him a birthday present he knew he would like. Except when it came to sports equipment, Peter wasn't much of a shopper, but in one of his forays to the athletic emporiums of Washington street he had gone into an antiques shop where he found a little silver flask, round in shape with a picture in scrimshaw on one side.

> *May 15, 1988: Today is my father's fifty-eighth birthday. If anyone seems to be fifty-eight, it's not him. When I think of fifty-eight, I think of golf clubs bowing outward under the weight of bald CEOs, waiting to tee off.*
>
> *Well, Dad isn't bald, and he'll never be a CEO, but he is fifty-eight. So what else is fifty-eight? It is the age that litters the obituaries. At the age of fifty-eight, after a long bout with blah, blah.*
>
> *Death crosses my mind, and it worries me. But more importantly, does it bother Dad? It's not the easiest thing to ask him. He has conceded to taking an aspirin every other day to keep cardiac arrest away. That makes me feel a little better.*
>
> *More than anything else though, fifty-eight is just two years short of sixty. And if Dad is sixty, what am I besides twenty-three? Am I proud that he still looks healthy? Am I patronizing toward him? Am I mad that my father, the only one I've got, is already sixty? Or am I just plain scared because the man whom I have always been able to lean on now has a hard time getting out of his chair?*
>
> *Well, I don't know any of the answers for an obvious reason. But I know I will be sad if I don't get a chance to find out.*

It looked as though Brooks might have to wait quite a while to receive his gift, because a Westminster friend, who lived near Boston, had suggested to Peter that they might drive to Oregon and back after Peter finished his exams. There was from the start a good deal of uncertainty as to whether this trip would actually take place.

> *May 24, 1988: Is there something wrong with not knowing if you're going to travel cross-country by car until a day before it happens or doesn't happen?*
>
> *John mentioned the idea of this continental trek over two months ago. From the outset, I liked the idea, but I also thought that comprehensive planning would be essential if such a trip was to occur. Well now, two months later, all I know is that, if John's car gets the mechanic's okay tomorrow, off we go.*

But something doesn't fit. Why doesn't the prospect of leaving for Oregon in two days when I haven't even thought of what to bring, scare the hell out of me? I'm certainly apprehensive but I'm not really that scared because if I were, I would be thinking about backing out. But I've mentally committed myself and that is the key. I may not know how much money to bring, how long it's going to take, or what would be the best bug repellent with which to face America, but I have prepared myself to be unprepared.

They did not go. Peter didn't say much about it except that he had been looking forward to seeing more of the country.

May 26, 1988: I'm not going to workout. I'm going to go home. I'm shunning my daily roughage and having pizza. Forget James Joyce. I'm going to read Sports Illustrated. *Bills were going to be paid. They will be paid but not until Monday. Only three cigarettes a day you say? Fine, I'll have my fourth at 12:01. So all of tomorrow you'll only have two. When is that? I'll dream about a girl I've never met. What about the ones you meet? They are not here now. Oxford is a month away. What about three weeks from now? It will be June 18th. You are at home now, right? No, I am home. I'm also done with exams. Do you understand? Yes. Will you be returning soon? I have to. Why? Because it's late and I need to sleep. Welcome back. Thanks. Who am I? I don't know but I'm used to you.*

Peter stayed home a couple of days and planned to return the next weekend so we let him take a car. "My independence welled up inside me," he wrote, "And found ultimate expression in the form of a two-door 1985 light blue buick. With every inch of Massachusetts I put between myself and Dad, the more the car felt like mine, at least for a week." Later he described himself leaving work at midnight with a bounce in his step at the thought of being home by 12:15. After scouring the side streets for more than half an hour looking for a place to park, he ended that day's entry with a typically rueful sentence. "I'm not sure I'm ready to have a monogamous relationship with any form of transportation."

The next weekend Peter brought the car home and on Sunday when Brooks was busy and I was not feeling well, he drove to Westminster to get Tom. Peter's new confidence was not such that he wanted to talk to his former teachers so he pushed Tom through the post-graduation lunch line faster than his brother would have liked. They ate quickly, packed the car and left before Tom had time to say all of his goodbyes.

Back in Boston the sun was out for good and it was getting hot.

Peter had plenty of time for golf and the Red Sox and sitting around with friends. The year before he had been worried about how to tell his friends about what he had been through without alienating them; now he was in a hurry to get back in line, to pick up the step, especially the social step that he felt he had begun to lose back at Westminster.

Peter was still finding it hard to make dates with girls and Wendy had cautioned him to relax and not attach so much importance to the ones he did make. But that June before he went to England he had no one on whom to practise this advice. While his own social life consisted of occasional beer parties and many evenings sitting around with Jeff and Mike, he remained the observer in the field of male/female relationships.

> *June 3, 1988: My roommate's friend, Sam, his girlfriend, Kelly, and her best friend are in town for an abortion.*
>
> *Kelly is having the abortion. I don't know how Sam and particularly Kelly feel about the situation. It interests me. Until now, due to my general lack of interaction with the opposite sex, my feelings about abortion have been framed by various contexts of media and sex education classes.*
>
> *But beyond the initial curiosity of seeing a societal buzzword unfold on a personal level, I'm greatly intrigued by the specifics of this abortion-to-be. For instance, on Wednesday night, I entered my apartment to the background sound of Wendy talking to Sam on the phone. I assumed the conversation had to do with the logistics surrounding the abortion. Not quite.*
>
> *Wendy: I don't know. Hold on. Peter, are the Red Sox in town this weekend?*

Me:(slightly taken aback by the question) Ah, yeah, well, yeah, they are.

Wendy:Peter says they are. Do you want me to pick up some tickets? Yes? How many? Is Kelly going to want to go? (Pause.) All right. I'll call you tomorrow.

It took me a moment to process the implications of that phone conversation. Then I said, "Oh, that's nice. Got to come to the city for an abortion. Might as well catch a ball game." In between giggles, Wendy said it wasn't funny. I got a good laugh out of it. The picture of Kelly standing up and spilling popcorn as she cheered for a home run just hours before getting a fetus sucked out of her was either absurdly incongruous or abrasively practical. The protection of having no personal stake in the matter allowed me to laugh.

Sam arrived in town on Thursday. Kelly and her friend weren't coming until Friday night. I was on the front stoop of my apartment building, looking for my key while trying not to drop my Hostess crumb cake, when Sam appeared around the corner and bounded up the steps. Having not fully absorbed the schedule surrounding the abortion, I was a little surprised to see him.

"Ah, Sam!? How you doing?"

In between chomps on a green apple, he replied, "Pretty good. Yourself?"

"Things will be better when I find my keys."

He laughed appropriately.

Later as I left for work, I started thinking about Sam. My first feeling was that he was acting oddly, but I strongly suspect that if he had just been up to party for the weekend, his behavior wouldn't have struck me at all. I definitely wanted to see some discernable manifestation of the impending abortion, but how is one meant to act less than two days before a vital expression of one's manhood is to be mechanically exhumed.

Would I have been more satisfied if Sam had arrived at our door, head cast down, unshaven and barely able to spit up a hello? Or he might have bellowed a hearty greeting out of a mouth whose corners met at the back of his head, a robust manner which would only have been a pathetic veil over his profoundly traumatized soul. But Sam was neither of these. I have a hunch he was just as curious as I was about how he should act.

June 12, 1988

"Eve has AIDS, you know," Jeff said.

I couldn't tell if Jeff was talking to Mike or myself. I was stoned and, consequently, operating at several levels below my usual awareness. It took me a moment or two to register a feeling about what Jeff had just said. That first, thought, was, "Oh my God, I've just shared a bong with a person who has AIDS." Right on the heels of this thought came the notion that Jeff, who was quite unstoned, was relying on my grass-induced paranoia to play a joke on me.

"She doesn't have AIDS. She can't have AIDS."

"Trust me, Peter. She has AIDS." Jeff spoke in a very convincing manner.

Mike, who was too stoned to even bother looking at me, said, "She has AIDS, Peter."

I believed them. I turned to Mike and, with pronounced melodrama, bellowed, "You let me share a bong with someone who has AIDS?!"

Mike, turning to me casually, said, "You can't catch AIDS from a bong. I took plenty of hits and I'm not worried."

I knew Mike was right but that didn't stop me from imagining that maybe due to the dry mouth I had from getting stoned I had, without noticing, ruptured a tiny, tiny blood vessel on the inside of my lip and that Eve had done the same, and that some of her blood had gotten on the bong mouthpiece and had entered my tiny, tiny blood vessel and now I was going to die of AIDS.

I've had enough experience with myself to know when I'm being paranoid, whether I'm straight or stoned. However, I'm much better at diffusing paranoia when I'm straight, which is one of the reasons that I don't smoke pot often. Nevertheless, this is a time when I was definitely stoned, and my paranoia, with the instincts of a wolf spotting the weakest member of a caribou herd, was primed to get the best of me.

I tried to handle this stalking paranoia by eliminating the source of its strength.

I blurted out, "There is no way she has AIDS."

Jeff, thinking the topic was over, turned his attention from the T.V., made a half turn in his swivel chair to where he was facing me, and said, "Eve has AIDS. You don't. Stop worrying about it!"

I'm going to end this piece. Why? Because Jeff was lying and I want to write something else.

On his last visit home before he flew to England, Peter brought his journal of the spring for us to read. It was the first time I had seen one of his brown notebooks. I sat in a chair by the sofa in the living room with my feet tucked under me and started reading. It was a warm June evening. Peter wandered in and out of the room, and as I read, I told him how much I admired his ability with words and which sketches I liked best. When I got to the last page, there was a date at the top and then three lines in the center. Peter could see what I was reading and said, in explanation for such an uncharacteristic attempt, that the words of a poem had just seemed to come into his head.

A brain pregnant with an idea,
A burden easy to incur,
But not so to defer.

In the summer of 1989 when I was rereading Peter's journals, rationing them a few pages at a time, I reached the page with the familiar three line fragment, then turned it to find a four line poem. It, too, was in the center. In his slightly rounded racing letters, Peter had written:

A force unfamiliar to me
Drives a boy to flail the air.
Two clouded eyes must stop to see
A crumbled boy who wants not to care.

I had no sense of having seen the poem before. Now it seems as though I must have looked at the four lines that night when Peter stood nearby. Perhaps I read them mechanically or hurriedly. Maybe the phone rang or the timer dinged in the kitchen. I was not scared for Peter then.

11

PETER DID A LOT OF WRITING IN HIS SIX WEEKS AT TRINITY COLLEGE. In a battered folder labeled "Oxford," I found his journal for the summer and the syllabus for the writing course. The topics for weekly assignments were relatively unconstraining starting with "Your Earliest Memory," the one which had led Peter to describe himself coughing from his crib to get my attention. This with other descriptions and stories plus a short play fill Peter's second brown plastic notebook.

Ongoing journal entries were to be handed in for commentary at the end of the seminar and I suspect that in the first week the instructor encouraged her students to try variations in their approach to these. After an initial diatribe about the behavior of parents with small children in airports, Peter described one of his first days in England by switching from first person narration to second.

> *July 1, 1988: In Boston, there are days when it rains. In Oxford, there are rainy days. There is a difference. And until today, you had never seen a rainy day. You were frustrated by rain. You had no right to get mad at it. In Boston, you get mad because the rain is imposing on what otherwise would be a fine day. Today the rain seemed so relaxed as it fell at a gentle angle to the ground, the drops*

steady but not deliberate, in no hurry. Today the rain was not imposing on anything; it simply was the day.

On the afternoon of July 5 Peter called home at a time when he thought I would be watching my favorite soap opera, but I was out. Brooks reported Peter's news. The program was turning out to be better for him than he had thought was possible; we would be surprised at how much he was enjoying sightseeing; he was sleeping in a room where a monk had slept three hundred years before. We were relieved and delighted in his behalf and he was surprised at himself. "I'm alarmed to find myself loving England much the way my parents do and I realize I probably didn't enjoy it so much in past visits just because my parents liked it so much," he wrote after he had made trips to Blenheim and to London.

After I missed the third of Peter's weekly calls he and Brooks set a time for him to call me. It conflicted with my usual Wednesday appointment to read at the Recording For the Blind studio and I was slightly annoyed that Brooks had not remembered this. As all was well with Peter I decided to keep my appointment and talk to him the following week. Later Brooks reproached me saying that Peter had been disappointed that I was not home.

I have speculated since about what, if anything, he particularly wanted to tell me. Was it about Erin, a girl he was currently pursuing or about a day he had spent in a Cotswold village not unlike the one Brooks and I had taken him and Tom to a few years earlier? Probably the latter. I had left them that day to walk up a hill towards a house in which I had stayed when I was in my twenties.

Most uncharacteristically Peter had found himself doing the same sort of thing. "I decided to follow a path I saw leading out of town and into the surrounding pastures. Once I'm alone, my fantasy mode takes over. It wasn't long after entering the fields that I started to picture myself as the "young American" on a quest to find himself via a carefree backpacking spree in Europe."

It was from Carolyn, who was visiting friends in Galway and went over to spend a week with Peter, that we first heard about Erin. Over a meal for which Carolyn was paying and at which Peter ate voraciously, ordering the entree twice, he encouraged her to pursue a young man she had just met in Galway and then described his attraction to Erin and his efforts to make headway with her. These ended in failure the following week leaving Peter a few days to wax more contemplative in his journal before embarking on another romance.

July 27, 1988: The more I learn about wallowing in self-pity, the less I enjoy it. I had a couple of pints tonight. I drank them quickly. Is that why I thought there might still be something between Erin and me? I'm not sure. First and foremost, I wanted to fool around with her again. But I took a roundabout approach.

"Do you regret that we decided just to be friends?"

Hell, that wasn't even the honest way to put it.

"Do you regret that you decided that we should just be friends?"

What did I want her to say to that?

As she moves closer to me, "I've thought about it a lot and maybe it wouldn't be so bad if we had some fun in the last couple of weeks."

Of course, I knew she wouldn't say that. But I let myself fantasize that she would. Physical drive aside, I did have something else I wanted to say to her.

"You misled me. Why the fuck did you do that? I don't give a shit that you were confused. How could we be so happy for two nights? Christ, you even wanted me to stay longer Saturday night. But I was a little nervous and thought it wouldn't be a crime to take it slow. And before I know it, we're just casual Sunday night, and by Monday, you went around the world to avoid me."

Of course, I didn't say it that way. But even if I had, what kind of answer was I expecting?

There is no answer. She said something anyway, though.

"If you weren't so nice, it probably would have gone on longer."

Is that meant to make me feel good? It doesn't. Can we go back two weeks? I'll be meaner, less considerate, insensitive. Jesus, I don't want to hear that some innate trait of mine is the reason I'm writing in this fucking thing instead of caressing you.

"Oh, but it was a good experience."

"Ah, fuck you. I can think of better experiences."

Why does she have to tell me that she's still very attracted to me? She wants just the two of us to have dinner before we leave. Great. I don't need an hour and a half of staring into those thunderstorm blue eyes and seeing that she feels for me. I will consider it, though, if she buys.

July 28, 1988: Bored with Trinity, bored for eternity. I don't think so. At least, I hope not.

I had so much time today. I bummed around like it was a rainy Sunday afternoon at home. The thing is, I still got a decent amount of work done. I did it in the morning, though, and had the whole rest of the day staring me in the face.

I could have written letters. I took a nap. I could have read. I played pool. I could have gone to the tourist information office. I watched an inane sitcom on T.V. And I was content doing what I did and what I didn't do. But perhaps, if you're satisfied with being bored, you're not really bored.

What a thought.

The night time picked up a little. There was the U. Mass seminar versus Trinity Staff dart challenge. We lost 8 to 4, but from what I understand, after I cut out, there was a pint match which we won. I wished I hadn't left. But it's like me to jump into the pool and scramble out (in spite of myself), even if I'm getting used to the water.

When I left, I went to shoot some more pool. I eventually ended having an enjoyable if pretentious conversation with Frank, the bartender, about the root of family instability in America.

July 29, 1988: I'm becoming a master napper. It doesn't seem to matter whether I'm tired or not. If I've got nothing better to do, or if I'm not ready to do something that I should, I simply drop in on my bed.

It's always there. It doesn't ask me any questions and it doesn't care how long I stay. If it had a face, it would have a gentle knowing smile on it. Because the bed knows that I'm the one who decides when to visit and, more importantly, I'm the one who decides when it's time to leave.

My bed is often better for me than my parents are. Mom and Dad know that I have to make my own decisions, but, ultimately, they're still my parents and always will be. They just can't stop themselves from butting in on my issues. It's annoying but I've accepted the fact that my mother will still want to know when I'm forty why I didn't bring more underwear. You accept this because you know that if you ever have kids you'll do the same shit. This is why everybody, at some point in their lives, preferably just after they've left the nest, should sleep in an objective bed that has a good sense of self. It definitely helps you develop some discipline outside the parental realm.

In his last week at Oxford Peter made himself think about returning to Boston and the challenge of starting classes at B.U. The School of Communications had not only accepted him but had encouraged him to transfer from U. Mass for the fall term rather than waiting until January. He had been pleased by their faith in his abilities but was anxious about the change.

August 2, 1988: The end of the seminar is coming on fast, each day consumed quicker than the previous. You can fight it or get in step with it. It's best to pursue the latter, to try to tap the effusive energy that characterizes the last moments of a good time.

This doesn't mean that you don't prepare yourself for the let down because there will be one, no matter how you chose to use the end.

Some people seem to want to take the edge off the let down. There is nothing wrong with that. But I don't think to accomplish this they should belittle the validity of an enjoyable month and a half.

"Oh, this has been fabulous, but it's not the real world."

Wrong. This has been as real as anybody's bills, job or school. It's been a very pleasant slice of the real world. It's not criminal to encounter one every so often.

So, how do you prepare for the letdown? I take little slivers out of the day, maybe five minutes or so, and I go back to Boston in my head.

So far, I've deboarded the plane in Logan and melted in the August heat, gotten to my apartment, and seen all the bills, gone to awkward orientation programs at B.U., and perhaps most difficult, I've gone to the library to research a paper.

I've gotten good results when I've done this in the past. It basically comes under the heading of, "If You Prepare For The Worst It's Usually Never As Bad As You Imagined."

Well anyway, I've got a few days left. I'm going to try to live them instead of trying to save them. And I'll probably go back to Boston a couple more times, but that leaves plenty of time to eat, drink and be perhaps a little wary.

Peter did not write about Catherine, a Canadian girl, until she had abruptly withdrawn from their brief but intense affair which took place in the final weeks of the program. It was Peter's first sexual encounter and although he did not understand Catherine's change of heart, he did not regret what he described to me on the phone as "two weeks of bliss." He had called to say that he would join a group of students from the program in an apartment in Edinburgh for the week after their classes ended. Catherine would be one of the group.

While they were in Edinburgh Peter was invited to spend a week in a villa outside of Barcelona owned by the family of one the girls with whom he was travelling. Catherine had already been invited and in spite of the offish way in which she had been treating him, Peter was tempted by the opportunity to stay at such a place.

August 16, 1988: (in Barcelona) I said my piece with Catherine. She was (or so she said) content to let our short but intense get-together drift into friendship without any heralding.

I can't deal with that sort of approach. I need to know where I stand, or I need to let the other person(s) know where I stand. If Catherine had been affectionate toward me when we got to Edinburgh, then I never would have said what I did. I just would have gone on trying to make inroads into her life and hoping that she would sleep with me at least a couple more times.

But it was fairly obvious that whatever we had she opted to leave behind at Trinity, which is alright but why couldn't she just tell me that instead of avoiding me for two days.

In some ways, though, it was a hidden blessing because it allowed me to get some perspective on the whole thing. I mean, I had said to myself at times, as the program was coming to an end, that it would be best for me to stop things with Catherine before I got attached only to go off to B.U. to forge my more permanent existence. The bottom line, though, was that if we could be together at night, make love and hold each other afterward, if there was any chance of that, then I was going to juice right to the last night we were together.

But it didn't happen that way, and I saw my opening, the right time to sit down and say, "It would be best for me, with starting at B.U. and all, to just be friends the rest of the trip."

She didn't like this, though. Why, I'm not sure. For one thing, I think she didn't enjoy being confronted by something she would just as soon have swept under the rug. I'd also like to think that she didn't expect this from me. She's a beautiful, desirable woman, and I'm sure she is used to having men at her disposal, at her whim. Well, I felt like I was at her whim for a while and, no matter how nice her body was, it wasn't worth it for only a week and maybe a few fucks. And now I don't have to worry if my underwear is clean.

August 17, 1988 I'm sitting on the veranda of a glorious two-hundred-year-old Spanish villa. I don't know the name of the town but that doesn't matter. It's somewhere outside of Barcelona.

When I was first invited to come here, the enticement was four more days with Catherine. The more I thought about it, the more I was excited just about coming here. And, at that point, I had no idea what I was coming to. Just the fact alone that we'd be within an hour and a half of the beach and that it was forever sunny and niney-two degrees was enough to get me in the mood.

This place, though, Casa Nova, has been enough to make me forget about the beach and almost enough to forget about Catherine.

The whole thing is something out of a movie. I'm walking through these high-ceilinged, breezy rooms with their tiled floors and opulent furniture. I'm swimming in the friendly waters of the pool.

I'm slipping into sleep on the porch sofa swing. I'm hitting serves on the immaculate tennis court. But am I really touching anything, affecting anything? Does the water ripple out when I jump in? Will I, never mind anybody else, ever believe I was here a month from now? I'll get pictures of this place and maybe I'll even be in them, but will I wonder whether that's me I see lounging by the pool or just somebody I know but rightfully can't get in touch with anymore and most likely, most suitably, never will.

This is a place and a time I will tell my kids about and they'll smile and be genuinely inquisitive, and yet, somewhere in the backs of their heads where cynicism is starting to burgeon, they'll look at old dad in his t-shirt and jeans and think, "no way." And I'll sense their disbelief or maybe just my own projected onto them, and I'll go off to find those pictures that would have been long gone were it not for my wife's thing about picture albums. And I'll show them the pictures and they'll believe it more than me.

Two days after he returned to Boston Peter came home for a doctor's appointment and stayed for about a week. He saw Jeff and a few other old friends and put up with Tom's often stormy behavior on the tennis courts. One evening when Brooks and Tom had gone off to a college interview, Peter and I had dinner alone. He told me more about Catherine. She had offered him a place to stay with friends of hers in London the night before they were to fly home and they had parted on better terms. He was able to look at her critically, saying that she was more selfish than he had thought at first. His sense of accomplishment and pleasure in his summer seemed to far outweigh his disappointment in the romance.

August 24, 1988: I'm at my parents house now, visiting where I lived for fourteen years. The last time I was here, I was acutely sensitive to the refuge dimension this place has played in my life. How it, at once, has been oh, so comfortable and yet, ultimately, so dangerous.

This time is different, though. Its comfort, and correspondingly its danger, seems to have faded into the background. I'm still aware of it and probably always will be, but I don't feel driven to around-the-clock, emotional, sentinel duty. Falling into the folds of deceiving warmth seems much less likely to happen to me on this particular journey.

Why?

Well, it has something to do with my success at Oxford. I turned it on when it counted, which puts my mind somewhat at ease. I passed an important test and realize, perhaps, that I don't always have to be making up little tests for myself, like I do when I visit my parents. Hey, kick back for a while. You've earned it, and you also know that soon enough you'll face a harder test that counts for more, B.U.

I guess maybe I'm starting to learn to get a feel for what my psyche needs, what's good, what's important and what's overkill, a harsh lesson that resulted in me stepping out of my head and back into life.

Peter who had seldom corresponded with anyone, accumulated that fall at least a dozen letters and cards from his friends in the Oxford program. The letter that surprised him most came from Catherine soon after she arrived home in Calgary. She apologized for her behavior especially in light of what she called, "Your past instabilities and insecurities," and encouraged him to send her some of his writing, "for constructive criticism or overwhelming praise."

"He wrote the funniest letters," Catherine said in a letter to Wendy after Peter died and then somewhere in the long and, by her own admission cathartic letter, she remembered, "I thought of him as the life of the party in a low-key sort of way."

12

In order to get himself in the right frame of mind for the "harder test" he anticipated at B.U. Peter went back to Boston a few days before their orientation activities were to start. He was beginning to think of the city as his home. However, the only person in his Boston home was Wendy who, because she had a full time job as well as classes, did not spend much time in their apartment.

Peter had only been back a few days when he noted in his journal that, "for the first time since Wendy and I have been roommates one of us brought home a date." Peter was accustomed to towering over others but John was taller than he and from their first awkward handshake over a kitchen chair, he was uneasy with him. As he would describe him, "John just stood there being big." From that night on Wendy spent most of her evenings with John and Peter became more than ever determined to find a more active social life at B.U.

> *September 7, 1988:*
> *"Oh, she's just a G.S.U. Rat."*
> *"What's a G.S.U. Rat?"*
> *"Somebody who hangs out at the G.S.U."*
> *"Oh…what's the G.S.U.?"*

"It's the student union. You've been there, haven't you?"

"Oh, yeah. I..."

"It's in the building we played pool in, right above it where we watched the Super Bowl."

"Right. Sure. Okay."

That short exchange seemed innocent enough when it occurred. Now, though, in light of my recent matriculation at Boston University, it's taken on a whole new meaning.

This transformation has occurred during the last three days' worth of lunches which I have consumed at the G.S.U. The first day, Wednesday, was the most gentle of the three afternoon repasts. This was due in large part, if not entirely, to the fact that I had lunch with Jeff (one of my few and definitely most familiar ports in the social storm that is B.U.).

Getting down to specifics, Jeff and I had agreed to meet for lunch at around 11:30. I arrived at twenty after, courtesy of one of the typically abbreviated first day's class. One of the first things I noticed as I entered the union, outside of the fact that Jeff had not yet arrived, was the number of people eating a meal at one time. Never in my life have I seen so many people in a school cafeteria. For me, this was fertile ground for surging feelings of low esteem.

Peter went back to his old job at a speciality food store, where he worked three or four evenings a week at the delicatessen counter and helped to close up. He was pleased with himself for having requested and received a modest raise in his hourly pay. But although his time at work provided him with company, it didn't count as "socializing" in Peter's version of the life he wanted to be leading.

September 11, 1988: I've got this feeling that it wouldn't take too much to lighten my mood. One call from Jeff or from Darren or a conversation with a nice girl at the G.S.U. would do the trick. It's important that I remember that it could take something as small as I've mentioned to feel a little less lonely. It helps to keep my feelings from overwhelming me. Because, after all, it certainly hasn't taken much to bring me down.

The weekend sucked, but that doesn't mean I sucked. I'm twenty-one, more ready this year to go out and make friends and take some risks than I was at this same time last year or at any other time in my life, for that matter. There weren't too many opportunities this weekend. To start with, I worked both Friday and Saturday nights. Now I'll be honest and admit that part of me likes it when I'm on for both nights of the weekend. It gives me a legitimate excuse for having a socially dead weekend. However, that part of me is growing smaller and smaller, and I have requested not to be put on the schedule for those two nights if at all possible.

Also, to be fair to myself, my particular relationship with B.U. is going to make it difficult to form any sort of bonds with new people. But that's the way it is, and I certainly don't want to use that fact as an excuse for not doing everything in my power to get involved with the B.U. flow and meet people.

Peter did not seem to feel that just attending his classes, four full time courses and an advertising lab, constituted a sufficient effort to meet people, so he signed up to work for the Dukakis campaign. When he told me about this plan on the phone I encouraged him. He had never done volunteer work before and I thought an inside look at a political campaign, in however menial a position, might interest him.

September 13, 1988:It was my first day volunteering for the Duke, and I was anxious to get started, to become part, in some way beyond voting, of a presidential campaign. Now I realized that by nature volunteer work was not going to put me into the thick of things, but I was expecting to work on what I had signed up for, which was phone polling and rallies. Silly me.

"This is a campaign. There is always something to do," announced Mike, the rotund and proportionately jovial head of the volunteer office, as I found myself marvelling at the number of bumper stickers and accompanying envelopes that could fit into a long abandoned Smirnoff's case.

"Well, how's that to start with? We've certainly got more of them."

"Actually...

"Great! I'll be over here if you have any questions."

Well, Mike seemed so goddamned happy about getting me and the bumper stickers together that I was intimidated at the prospect of asking him about doing some telephoning instead. So I sat down with the bumper stickers and the envelopes and tried giving myself an impromptu pep talk on the innate virtues of being a "team player." In less than twenty minutes, and who cares how many stuffed envelopes later, I felt lower than a water boy.

September 19, 1988: Having gotten a taste of the envelope-stuffing end of the volunteer business, I decided, previous to arriving for my second stint at campaign office, that I would take some initiative, make my way past the envelope man, and head upstairs to where the phone polling is done. Before I knew it, I was clasping hands with the head of polling, who also happened to be named Peter.

"Peter, how'd you like to come over to campaign headquarters and help me bring back the new polling surveys?"

"Yeah, sure."

Stuffing what...I'm on my way to Dukakis For President National Headquarters.

At the Dukakis volunteer headquarters, the receptionist gets excited if somebody passing by on the street so much as glances out of the corner of their eye through the office window. At National Campaign Headquarters, you can't even get into the main hallway without passing a security checkpoint monitored by the most Republican-looking of thugs.

Peter, of course, had security clearance for me, as long as I promised to stay by his side the whole time. I felt strangely complimented by this conditional entry.

Well, once inside, we headed straight for a small staircase tucked in the back corner of the front hallway. It led down to the cellar. Five floors worth of headquarters and we head right for the basement. Why?

"This is where all the action is," offered Peter in a suspiciously upbeat tone as if he had bugged my thoughts.

However, once we entered the basement offices, I was moved to reconsider the motivations of Peter's enthusiasm for the nether regions of campaign headquarters. To put it simply, the "gender gap" was enticingly evident. And many of these beautiful, young campaigners seemed to be familiar with Peter, who, in greeting some of them, lost any apparent knowledge of my dogging presence. I noticed that the female campaigners not only did not return my hello's but seemed intent on slamming me into desks or, in the case of some of the bigger girls, laying tracks of heel marks down my back on their way to file this or that or to say hello to Peter.

Peter finally got his chance at the phones and even completed the six page, twenty-eight question survey a few times. One evening he called to entertain us with an imitation of the responses of a lady he had polled in Tennesee. But by September 27th he lamented in his journal, "I don't get that feeling of being part of a team." He concluded his entry with the statement: "Phone polling is a self-inflicted torture and would be even if my fellow pollers greeted my every completed survey with cheers."

I don't know if Peter ever went back to volunteer again because the next page in his journal notebook is dated January 1, 1989. That is the page Carolyn and I turned to in the motel room the week after he died. In the intervening months Peter wrote the long memory piece about the November night two years before when he had told Brooks and me he wanted to disappear. I believe the only person who knew he was working on this description was Catherine, who said in her letter to Wendy, "I called him a few months ago...It sounded like he was adjusting to B.U. very well...feeling secure about himself...He told me he was beginning to write about his experiences when (to quote him) he was 'in the dumps.'"

I saw Peter only once in Boston before he came home for Thanksgiving but he called at least once a week and I sensed in our conversations his need to feel that his life was on a par with those of his friends, most of whom would graduate in the spring. He had plans to get an internship for the summer with a newspaper or TV station. Among his papers I would find a list of about a dozen job descriptions with names of the persons he should contact and the dates at which applications would be accepted. But it was with greater urgency that he expressed his desire for a more active social life, in particular, a girlfriend. Some of his friends, including Jeff, already had serious relationships with girls. Peter admitted that his quest for a girlfriend had become the main subject of his sessions with Dr. Rhodes.

November 2, 1988 was Peter's twenty-second birthday. I had a class that evening but Brooks went to Boston and took Carolyn and Peter out to celebrate. He told them over dinner that he was about to have his last appointment with Dr. Rhodes. Apparently it had been agreed when Peter returned from Oxford that he would continue therapy only until he had had a chance to get adjusted to B.U.

In the eighteen months since Peter's discharge from McLean's, he and Dr. Rhodes had met weekly and their relationship appears to have become a pleasant one with little push or pull. They started by talking about Peter's anxieties about getting off his medication, (he wanted to be free of it) and getting into jobs and classes. Later most of their talk revolved around Peter's social life with Dr. Rhodes suggesting ways in which Peter could anticipate the situations which made him uneasy and plan ahead as to how to handle them.

Dr. Rhodes' entries for his final two sessions with Peter read almost as though Peter had taken on the role of a protegee who has mastered a skill and is about to take it out into the world.

> 10/27/88-Says he has learned a lot and almost finds it hard to remember what those months of lethargy at home two years ago were about.

> 11/3/88 I reiterate my ongoing availability—that I'd like to hear from him from time to time. (He) speaks of what he sees ahead academically and socially. Feels he'll be carrying me with him as, "What Dr. Rhodes would say." And will let me know how things go.

A few weeks later Peter had told us that the only the thing he missed about therapy was not having "someone to tell my successes to." Whatever Dr. Rhodes intended, he had bidden farewell to a Peter who would not return to him unless he had a trophy to display, who would not ask him for the help he thought he should not need. I would conclude in my journal that, "He (Dr. Rhodes) came in far into the story and never understood the plot."

Dr. Rhodes did not hear about Cynthia. She invited Peter and another boy from the Oxford program to visit her at Columbia early in November. Peter had seen her in Boston once before she left for college and they had exchanged a few letters. Cynthia evidently knew about Peter's involvement with Catherine, because she had sent him a set of pictures from the summer including, "for posterity's sake," one of him with Catherine. I don't know what hopes Cynthia had for the weekend visit but certainly Peter was completely surprised by their attraction to each other. As he would put it. "I wouldn't like to have been the other guy."

Peter left us on Saturday of Thanksgiving weekend to take Cynthia out in Boston and in December made another weekend visit to Columbia.

13

PETER LIVED JUST TWELVE WEEKS INTO HIS TWENTY-THIRD YEAR. AS the date of his birth approached in 1989 I started to think in terms of the dwindling days on which I could reach back a year and find him alive, then write in my journal of what I thought he might have been doing on a particular date in 1988.

On November 2, I was alone. Brooks was in Boston on that day. As soon as his garden was battened down for winter, he had begun to spend several days in the middle of each week at his apartment. On those days I would stay as long as possible at the Recording for the Blind studio then do a few errands in town. On my return home I often sat in my car in our driveway contemplating the hours stretching ahead of me until two a.m. when I could count on falling asleep with the help of a pill. I studied, as though they were unfamiliar, a low wall in front of my car, a scraggly birch tree still holding a few yellow leaves and the locked back door. There was no motion.

The hour between four and five had always been tea time. In the blank kitchen window I could picture Brooks and me, ten or fifteen years earlier, sitting at the round table, impatiently telling whichever child appeared in the doorway to just let us finish a few sentences, please. When the car grew too cool, I got out, collected a package or two and went in to turn on some lights in the stillness, to make myself a cup of tea and a piece of toast. I took these, as I would later take my evening meal, to my chair in the bedroom in front of the TV. If I watched something—almost anything would do for a while—I would not consume the toast with honey or cinnamon so fast. With such comforts I could divide the hours until they began to move ahead on their own, until I felt myself dozing off in front of some program I had deliberately chosen, a documentary or a once loved movie. I watched or rewatched World War Two in fact and fiction for hours on end that year, acutely aware, as I sat in my comfortable chair, of how the scenes of wholescale destruction dwarfed Peter's singular death.

When Brooks was home the house, which even with one less room had for many years contained five people, seemed too small for the two of us. He said, only half joking, that he needed to build another wing for himself. And on the evenings when my mind could find no place to go that it could stand to be I wished that he had such a place. I would walk and scream and then drive and scream, in the dark, on roads I'd never seen, until, back at a familiar crossroad, fear and exhaustion would head me home to a pill and some sleep.

After such a night I would wake between nine and ten o'clock to hear Brooks preparing to leave for a few days in Boston. If it were not a day on which he had planned the trip then I knew that my acts of desperation had made him go. I always came out to the kitchen to say good-bye and watch his car turn out the drive to the left and head for the turnpike.

By midmorning I pictured him stopping for coffee at one of the familiar restaurants. He would meet Carolyn for lunch if she were in the city on one of her part time jobs and then go on to the Massachusetts Historical Society, the place he had been going to on the day when he gave Peter a last hug at the

Mass. Avenue T stop. He had begun to try to reimmerse himself in a research project he had started on just before Peter died. On his way home he would stop for tea with my mother. I could certainly imagine them in that big dark living room.

Things had changed in that house since I had left my mother standing alone in the hall a year earlier. Upstairs in one of the guest rooms my father was dying, bewildered and offended that an operation for cancer in the summer had so fatally weakened him. Much of the time he did not want to see anyone, not even my mother. Fortunately she was distracted to some degree by the comings and goings of my sisters and the nurses and household helpers they had hired when my father became too frail to resist. I wanted to hear about it all when Brooks called at night. It was a diversion, like reading the sequel to a book whose characters' every reaction I could anticipate. I even envisioned a role for myself, as I would have behaved if Peter had not died, the eldest daughter part in which I was so well practised. "I'm missing a rite of passage," I wrote in my journal, but I could feel the screams rising from somewhere deep within at the very thought of entering that house.

On the days when I caught sight of the top of Brooks' car as I came along our road, I remembered my old feelings of unalloyed pleasure in the fact that he was home from one excursion or another. That feeling was gone; I was simply relieved that he had negotiated the turnpike safely one more time. For four or five days until his next leave-taking we would live around each other, following almost imperceptible routines.

In the late afternoon he would call out to me to ask if I wanted a cup of tea and I would accept, the habit so ingrained that for a half hour we could sit and talk. He complained that at times I repeated myself in mindless fashion and easily forgot the stories he brought back from his forays in town, the lapses appearing to bother him as much as my excesses of accuracy had in the past.

Sometimes he deliberately saved a story for dinner time

or I might prompt one by asking what he had talked about with friends at lunch. Once when I did this, he misunderstood and snapped, "Well, we didn't talk about Peter."

Talking about Peter and not talking about Peter produced an equal heaviness between us, while for me talking about him to others could lighten the weight of his death as though the listener were carrying it with me for a space. Brooks hated to hear me in these conversations on the phone, yet he admitted that he envisioned some ideal person, one he could not name, with whom he would someday like to speak of his relationship with his older son.

One night when we were not able to avoid a descent into Peter's life, when the conversation went on through dinner time and beyond, Brooks finally retreated to his chair in the living room. I stood in the doorway and watched his long features twist as he said in response to one of my endless speculations, "The point is we lost him."

Tom came home to what he called, "this bastion of memories," on a couple of weekends in October and when he was here the tension between Brooks and me relaxed a little. After dinner as I restlessly rose to clear the table, he and Brooks would sit talking, smoking and sipping Tom's favorite red wine. Then late at night he sometimes came into Carolyn's room, as he had in the summer, to sit on the floor and talk to me about Peter. One night he remembered a conversation at Westminster the year before when one of the teachers had asked how Peter was doing and he had answered, "He's doing better than I am."

On the Tuesday before Thanksgiving I waited for Tom at the railroad station in Albany, watching as other college students greeted their parents with hugs and smiles and hurried away. Then he was suddenly beside me, leaning to kiss my cheek. He dropped his duffle on the floor, muttered something about cigarettes and walked off. I observed him almost as though he were not my son. He was taller and, if possible, thinner, his face pale and his chin dark with a stubble of growth which could not have been there the year before. It seemed as if he had covered more than ten months of the four years between himself and his brother. He was moving into a space between the sons I had in my mind.

We did not celebrate that Thanksgiving day. Carolyn stayed in Boston with friends and did not come home until Friday. Tom slept into the early afternoon and when he rose I warmed him up a lunch from the leftovers of a chicken dinner. He sat at the dining room table mixing all the food together on his plate in a way Peter had liked, saying that that was one of the places he could picture his brother most clearly.

A little later I looked out the kitchen window and saw him walking up near the road carrying a football he had bought the day before. I knew he was going to throw it towards a spot where Peter had stood waiting to catch another ball on Thanksgiving day a year earlier. Wherever it landed he would bury it. I did not watch the process. When he came back in the house he said he would do the same every year and I imagined a patch of footballs someday emerging from among the pines.

Over that weekend the four of us agreed not to try to go away for Christmas and sit marooned amid the festivities of others. Carolyn pointed out that our first Christmas without Peter could not be just another Monday and in the end she would be largely responsible for seeing that it wasn't.

One evening early in December Brooks asked me for the Christmas pictures. They were still in an envelope at the back of our latest album. I had not been able to decide whether or not to paste them into place after those of the boys throwing the football at Thanksgiving. Brooks took the envelope and sat in the living room for quite a while. I did not go in. I could not look at him looking at pictures of Peter or that powerful set of images of the way we were on Christmas day in 1988.

On December 24th, Peter and Carolyn arrived in Lenox at noon in Liz's car with Peter at the wheel and she a little annoyed that he had been able to pester her into letting him drive a borrowed car. They each showed me what they had bought for the other: silver earrings for Carolyn and a shirt Peter had picked out for himself in Quincy market. "Expensive," Carolyn said, but they had had fun shopping together.

Peter was the first to get his packages wrapped and placed under the tree. One was a large, oblong box for me, several pieces of decorated paper carefully taped together to cover it. My guesses as to what it could be were obviously wide of the mark, and Peter was amused. He had never taken such care with his gifts before, usually letting Carolyn or me wrap them.

Dinner on Christmas Eve was the only occasion of the year for which, as a family, we dressed up to eat at home. That year was not an exception, although by then our concepts of dressing up varied considerably. According to our custom I roasted a lamb and mashed the potatoes it had been Peter's job to peel. We congregated in the living room for hors d'oeuvres and ate by candlelight at a table Carolyn had decorated with greens and colored balls left over from the tree.

Sometime later in the evening, we continued a ritual that the children had long outgrown but did not want to abandon. Brooks, sitting in his accustomed chair—no one, of course, on his lap anymore—read *The Night Before Christmas* aloud. We four sat more or less in a circle around the room, amused glances flickering between us as we waited to hear the long-standing oddities of "Mam-a" in her kerchief and St. Nick's "cursers" flying to the rooftops.

When Brooks got to "Happy Christmas to all and to all a goodnight" and closed the thin, red book with its Arthur Rackham drawings, Peter, sitting on the floor against an over-stuffed chair, suddenly said, "You know, the five of us are lucky to be here. Not everyone has this." I was startled at first by his seriousness, and then said, "Yes."

The moment passed. Carolyn, Peter and Tom each took an old ski sock to the mantle in the other room and, heeding their father's request, tried to find old thumbtack holes from which to hang them.

A little later, Brooks and I were surprised to hear the phone ring. One of the boys answered it upstairs and, thinking that it must be my mother or a sister, I started up the steps. Tom called down that it was Cynthia. Brooks said, "On Christmas Eve?"

The next evening, we were in old clothes eating leftovers amid decorations and opened packages. The putter, which had emerged from Peter's box for me, was in the living room where I had practiced hitting balls along the carpet. Peter promised to christen it with me in the spring. He was more patient with my bad golf than either Brooks or Tom.

We took pictures in front of the Christmas tree which stood by Brooks' desk tied to the bookcase. It was, as always, a wonderful mess of a tree, lit with many colors, tinselled and hung with ornaments that served as a scrapbook of past Christmases—from the curling paper of a kindergarten angel to the benign smile of a cloth one reclining on the top branches. There is a staged picture of the three children in a roughhouse, all arms and legs, with Peter's face grinning from the floor. In others, the cat leaps out of Carolyn's arms and then from mine. The dog stares solemnly in front of Brooks and then Peter. We look ridiculously happy.

In the week before the new year, Carolyn went back to her job at Quincy Market, and Peter and Tom divided their time between TV and typing. Although there was always a trail of lettuce, cheese, ham and mayonnaise from the sandwiches they fed on while watching TV, they both actually did quite a bit of work.

Tom, working on college applications, moved between his room and the computer which was set up in the living room. Brooks sat in his chair trying to read the *New York Times* between interruptions to check Tom's essays and to give Peter facts from news articles. Peter walked around the room taking notes, then repaired upstairs to the typewriter to write them up as practice for his second term journalism course. Afterwards, he and Brooks would go over his pieces. Peter made notes along the margins, marking some statements as "editorializing."

For exercise, the boys played with the orange Nerf basketball Peter had given Tom along with a plastic hoop. That hoop, like so many before it, broke, adding to the scratch marks along the balcony, where for years Peter had devised ways of attaching hoops and bent hangers. Brooks used to ban these games at times, when the jumping stopped his antique clocks. But now that the boys were home together so seldom, he was more resigned; the carriage clock on the mantle and the grandfather clock in the corner were silent for a few days.

One morning I saw Peter jogging on the lawn in front of the house, a woolen cap stretched tight on his large head and our young, black Lab bouncing beside him on a leash. I said I liked the sight of them, but Brooks was worried. He had seen a note in Peter's room which read, "Run with Barry." When he told me about this on one of our walks, I felt a familiar tug of fear.

Writing reminders of what little efforts he could make in a given day had been Peter's habit two years earlier when he was struggling with depression. Now he seemed so different to me, more engaged in life than he had ever been before. I thought of him on Christmas morning, specifically stating that he was glad he could enjoy his presents and remembering how, two years earlier, he had seen life "from the bottom of a toilet bowl."

I reasoned with Brooks that it might be a long time before Peter would stop worrying about too much free time at home.

Peter must not have brought his journal notebook home with him because he used a piece of the yellow legal pad, on which he was making notes from news articles, to write an entry for December 29. In the upper left-hand corner, he wrote the word 'lonely', underlining it and leaving out the 'e'.

> *December 29, 1988: I've been home for five full days now. Is home the right word for it? I'm not sure. The saying goes, "Home is*

where the heart is." That timeless adage doesn't apply to me. At this point in my life, home is a place where I can balance myself emotionally, where there are chances for personal growth. Boston is my home now, in terms of those criteria.

In fact, increasingly I wonder what the attraction is of coming back to see my parents in the place that I used to call home.

I'm tempted to say that this house in the Berkshires and everything it entails and implies never offered me opportunities for personal growth. But the truth is the context of my family encouraged growth. The problem was when it was time to take what I had learned from my family into the world, or at least into the town of Lenox, I didn't do it.

I didn't move outside of my head and my family until I was away from Lenox. Because of this, I decided that Lenox and my parents' house would never be a place from which I could get anything accomplished.

So, if I associate this house with emotional, and at times, literal inertia (MTV), why do I come here and spend a week over Christmas rather than going back after, say two days?

As I passed under the stairs one day in mid-week, I heard Peter discussing with Tom how long he might stay at home. I called up to ask if he was thinking of asking Cynthia out for New Year's Eve, adding that in my day, it was considered important to have a date for that night. Peter called Cynthia right away and she accepted.

For the next couple of nights, Peter went to meet friends for drinks after dinner and I waited for his heavy step in the hall. He saw the light under our door and came in to tell us about whomever he had seen, leaning down first by my bedside then by Brooks' to kiss us good-night.

Brooks told me Peter sounded very pleased when he reported a further conversation with Cynthia to plan their evening. They had decided to have dinner, then go to the First Night celebrations on the Boston Common.

On Peter's last evening at home, Tom skipped dinner, partly because he had to finish an application to be mailed the next day, and partly because he didn't like the meatloaf Peter had requested. I thought I had made enough for Peter to take some back with him, but as he took his third helping, I could see that that was not going to happen. Between servings, Peter heeded Brooks' suggestion that he might need a dinner reservation in Boston on New Year's Eve, and went to the phone twice. He called his favorite French restaurant on Newbury Street, found that they had two time slots left and booked a table for nine o'clock. A few minutes later, he decided he and Cynthia might want to start earlier and, without cancelling his first booking, made one for six o'clock in her name. We watched with amusement, and a certain amount of wonder, Peter's approach to his first New Year's Eve date.

At about midnight, when Peter passed by the living room in his underwear on his way to bed, Tom was still working. He remembers that he barely looked up as they said good-night.

On Saturday morning, December 31, Tom was asleep, having stayed up most of the night to finish the essay which ended with the words, "I admire my brother." Peter was up early. After breakfast, he lugged his black duffel to the kitchen. For a few minutes, he stood in front of the sink in his new, navy blue, down jacket, talking to us. Then he leaned and kissed me goodbye.

Brooks drove him into Lenox and left him outside the town hall to wait for the 9:10 bus to Boston.

14

WHEN PETER LEFT THAT MORNING I AM CERTAIN THAT HE WAS AS innocent as we were of what was going to happen to him. He called Carolyn in the early evening to say that Cynthia hadn't appeared and he wondered if she had stood him up. But she hadn't. They went to the French Restaurant and then walked hand in hand among other First Night revelers on Boston Common. When he called a couple of days later Peter told me he had liked the feeling of being, "just like so many other people."

Yet by the time he said that he had already written of the morning of January 1, "A lot of free time was ahead of me and what I dread most about my life in Boston was staring me in the face—loneliness."

Through his diary, through Carolyn's eyes, Brooks' and my sister Isabella's, I have so many pictures of Peter in the first twenty-four days of 1989 that I find it hard to believe I did not see him. On Thursday of the bitterly cold first week of that month, Brooks delivered the computer on which Tom had been writing his applications back to Peter. He had bronchitis and was alone in the apartment. When Brooks got home he told me he had seen, "that trapped look in Peter's eyes."

I went right to the telephone.

"I'm glad you called, Mom." I heard need in Peter's husky voice. "You know when you want something and then when you get it, you're not so sure you want it?"

He had just heard that the dorm room would be available to him for the coming term. I was surprised. I had presumed that his off-campus apartment was an easier living arrangement for Peter than a dormitory would be and had no idea that he had put in a request to the B.U. Housing Office back in November. As we talked I was carefully non-commital, leaving unasked questions like: "Why did you want to move in the first place? What is wrong with living in your apartment with Wendy?" Instead I fussed about his health and persuaded him that it was too cold for him to go to work.

When he called the next morning, Peter's voice was still heavy but he sounded less tense. He was going to escape his apartment and go to my parents' house for the night. I was glad to hear that and said I'd call him there later to see how he was doing.

In the evening I traced Peter down at Carolyn's apartment where she was getting him something to eat before she went out. He described his reception at my parents' house. Knowing that my mother was expecting him, he had stood under the large portico ringing and ringing the bell only to be turned away when my father finally come to the door. I was sorry that Peter did not have the comfort of an evening with my mother and disappointed but not surprised by my father's reaction on hearing him cough. I said as much to Peter. We were both familiar with my father's determination to barricade himself against a wide range of ills.

The rest of our conversation was desultory but I attributed that more to Peter's health than to the fact the the dorm decision was closing in on him. I must have used the phase "total stranger" when referring to the roommate he had not been able to reach.

When Tom called Carolyn that evening from Westminster and got his brother instead, he sensed that Peter was low. They, too, discussed the option of the dorm room and Tom encouraged Peter to take it.

In the morning Peter got up and left Carolyn's apartment early. She was worried about him and asked him to call her in the evening. He did this from a stadium where he had gone with friends to see a hockey game assuring her he was alright.

When the phone rang at about ten the following night I turned off the television, crossed our room and stretched out on my bed expecting to talk to one of the children. Peter must have said something first that I don't remember, because a sensation of fear came before I heard the words, "My face was tingling, Mom. The whole bit."

He was describing the anxiety attack which had assailed him as soon as he decided not to accept the dorm room.

"That's not good, Pete." I tried not to react too much for his sake or my own, I'm not sure. I suggested that he should call Dr. Rhodes.

"Not yet," he said, I don't want to do that yet."

He had had a sense of having watched himself, and I asked if he thought that had helped him to get through the attack. He didn't know. I allowed myself to think it had.

Our conversation went on. He'd been to Isabella's for a small dinner party made up of Carolyn, Liz, his three first cousins, and a cousin of theirs, a boy just Peter's age. Peter identified this boy to me and asked if he were the one whose father had shot himself a month before. I said, "Yes." He expressed admiration for him, but we did not pursue the subject.

I told Peter I would call him the next night and he said he understood why but that he didn't want me to. I acquiesced saying that Brooks and I were coming to Boston later in the week.

Peter's voice dropped and slowed as he concluded, "Well, I've stood eight months in this place I guess I can stand four more."

I said I thought he could.

I went shopping for nightgowns in Boston the next

Wednesday afternoon and then because the store was relatively uncrowded I lingered, as I seldom do, to look at other things. As a result it was nearly five when I climbed the hill from the T stop, crossed the street and walked into my parents' driveway. Brooks was already at the house. My mother said that Peter had called around four but had decided not to come over when he heard that neither Brooks nor I were there. He had said he would call again before he left for work.

Soon I was sitting in the dark, high-ceilinged living room, the lamp behind me forming the only pool of light. My mother had just returned from one of her innumerable trips to the kitchen or pantry bringing things for tea, when the phone rang in the hall. I could hear Brooks talking and knew it was Peter. They were discussing grades and arranging to have lunch the next day. I was not thinking about Peter's Sunday call when Brooks motioned me to the phone.

I congratulated Peter on his marks but that was not what was on his mind. He wanted me to make sure that he could have lunch alone with his father, that Carolyn would not join them. I assured him he could, without asking why it was so important to him, without really asking how he was feeling at all. I was concentrating on getting back to having tea and talking to my mother.

As we drove home on Friday Brooks described his lunch with Peter in some detail. Peter had looked out the window of the restaurant and commented on the general dreariness of the gray day, the dispirited look of passersby. But he ate well. They discussed his decision not to take the dorm room and his recent bouts of anxiety. Brooks told him that he didn't think it would have been easy to move into a dorm at midyear and twice suggested that Peter talk to Dr. Rhodes. Peter resisted this idea, or at least wanted to postpone it.

After lunch, they walked up Newbury Street towards Massachusetts Avenue. Peter had to get home to clean his room in preparation for Cynthia's visit. At the entrance to the subway, Peter asked his father for a hug. Brooks sensed that it was not a casual request. He hugged Peter and watched him go down the dingy steps.

Brooks and I talked about that hug. Asking for such gestures of physical comfort had started as part of Peter's depression but had continued even as he recovered. It seemed a part of the more demonstrative Peter. I was more interested in the fact that Cynthia was coming.

I did not hear from Peter directly about this visit but he told his father that he had liked waking up and finding Cynthia there.

Classes started at B.U. the next week and remembering how restless Peter had been in the long break between terms the winter before, I was sure that he would be glad to get back to them. In our next conversation Peter told me he had decided to drop a history course in favor of one in abnormal psychology. I said it sounded like a good idea, thinking as I spoke that he might need to better understand all he had been through.

On Monday evening, a week into the term, I reminded Brooks, as we sat in the living room before dinner, that it was January 23, the date on which we had taken Peter to McLean's two years before. I reviewed with satisfaction all the progress Peter had made. A few hours later, after I had listened from across our bedroom as Brooks talked to Peter, I accepted without reservations his comment that Peter's voice sounded better, more "up," than it had in the last few weeks.

In those weeks Carolyn, Tom, Brooks and I had each been exposed to aspects of Peter's mood. Brooks saw the trapped look in his eyes when he was alone in his apartment with bronchitis. I heard the fear in his voice as he described his anxiety attack. Carolyn wondered why he was wearing his dirty old ski jacket instead of the new one he had shown off at Christmas. Finally on the last Monday Tom heard the dead sound in his brother's voice, "like that Christmas in Dublin," when they talked about Peter's difficulties with the computer program being used in his journalism class.

Only two hours later in talking to Brooks as I listened, Peter had passed lightly over this problem saying he'd been told he could just use a typewriter. Was he hiding his sense of panic from his father or did he for a moment believe that he would get by the problem in this way?

From his earliest years Peter had devised methods to combat his low tolerance for tension. Pursuading himself that something was not important was one and avoiding or leaving uncomfortable situations was another, until at Ithaca the very act of escape cast on him the humiliation he had so long kept at bay. At McLean's he thought he had learned his lesson. From the day when he called and said he thought he could, "get something out of this place," until he turned down the B.U. dorm, he did not allow himself to avoid a challenge.

In his talk with Tom he set a trap for himself. By that time his physical agitation was such that he could not imagine understanding the new computer program yet dropping a course in the subject he had chosen as his major was a defeat he could not accept.

Tom sounded a warning bell to his father the next afternoon and Brooks relayed to me that Peter had sounded bad. I did not call Peter and that omission, of course, haunts me, but not as much as does my reaction to the conversation I had with him two weeks earlier.

Sometimes when I'm lying on my bed, I stare at the blue telephone beside me and I can hear Peter's voice. "My face was tingling, Mom. The whole bit like the night you took me to the emergency room."

I let him persuade me that he could "handle it" when what I had to do was to see him, break into the painful constriction of his thinking and confront him with what we both knew of where his anxiety attacks could lead him.

I see Peter wearing the old ski jacket I took out of the cleaning bag on that cold August night in 1986. The night of January 24, 1989 was no colder. Is that why he chose the old jacket over the heavier new one or was he going back in time? He stands at the T-stop nearest his apartment on Commonwealth Avenue, a place I pass when I drive to where Carolyn now lives. At Arlington street he climbs the steep steps and walks with his shoulders hunched, up one block and across the street to the Plaza. I wonder if the desk clerk saw the trapped look in his eyes as he paid cash for his room. It cost about ninety dollars. Ordinarily he would have used a credit card. He must have stopped at a cash machine but I can't picture where. He crosses the lobby to the elevators, a familiar route which Brooks has been back to retrace. He enters the small room and puts his duffel on the bed. Then I transpose his pacing figure from the hallway off the emergency room in Pittsfield to the hotel room where he has less space. He could not have paced there for nine hours so he must have lain on the bed at times, but I only see him moving. The figure is still Peter's until it reaches the window; then, as in a dream, it becomes just a shape.

More than any time in his early years when I may not have heard Peter calling, it is my self-protective retreat in his last weeks which tips the balance scale of responsibility towards me in a way I cannot and do not even want to try to deny. Those who would divest me of responsibility for Peter's suicide would also divest me of responsibility for his life. There is no convenient dividing line. Unless I take such responsibility I have no right to be proud of Peter, proud of him for his absolute decency, even when he was miserable and mishandled, proud of him as he fought alone and lost alone, his final battle for life.

The unfamiliar force which Peter named in his poem had been with him since his crisis at Ithaca, threatening his life as an undertow threatens the lone swimmer practising a stroke he has been assured will carry him in the surf. Too often, the swimmer is not sufficiently persuaded of the danger below the waves. And no more are the watchers until they see the swimmer borne away.

15

On the afternoon of Christmas day in 1989, Brooks, Carolyn, Tom and I drove up into the graveyard. It was the first time the four of us had gone there since the day after Peter's burial when we had laid a bunch of flowers sent by his friends on the newly raked earth.

I leaned down to pick up a few pieces of blue wax from the candle I had packed into the snow the night before. It had burned in the cold stillness, illuminating the inscription on Peter's headstone. After dinner Tom had driven up to see if it was still lighted. It was. He said he could see it from the road as he approached.

Brooks placed a wreath at the foot of the stone and one of us said, "That's nice." He put a hand out and touched the top of the stone with the tips of his fingers. Then we turned, all at the same time, abruptly, and stood for a moment with our backs to Peter's grave and to each other.

There have been four more Christmases now, four more trips to the cemetery but it is only that first one that I remember, the picture in my mind becoming frozen as though someone had filmed it from above lifting the camera slowly away from the pattern we made as we turned.

We speak less often of Peter now as we gather to observe new holiday rituals. Over the years I have talked enough, always separately, to Brooks, Carolyn and Tom to know that we each carry in our minds different visions of Peter's final battle, different concepts of our powers to have changed its outcome and different beliefs about its power over our lives. That it has such power we do not question. We are learning to be careful with each other, to be wary of the spaces between us in the snow.